# ONE
# VOICE,
# SACRED
# WISDOM

# ONE VOICE, SACRED WISDOM

REVEALING ANSWERS TO SOME OF
LIFE'S GREATEST MYSTERIES FROM
YOUR GUIDES, SPIRITS, AND ANGELS

## JAMES SCHWARTZ

A division of
The Career Press, Inc.
Wayne, N.J.

ONE VOICE, SACRED WISDOM
Edited by Roger Sheety
Typeset by Kara Kumpel
Cover design by Amy Rose Grigoriou
Cover image by quinky/shutterstock
Printed in the U.S.A.

To order this title, please call toll-free 1-800-CAREER-1 (NJ and Canada: 201-848-0310) to order using VISA or MasterCard, or for further information on books from Career Press.

The Career Press, Inc.
12 Parish Drive
Wayne, NJ 07470
www.careerpress.com

**Library of Congress Cataloging-in-Publication Data**

CIP Data Available Upon Request.

# Acknowledgments

I want to extend my sincere gratitude to all of those people who volunteered to participate in these sessions. It is through your generosity that this incredible wisdom has been brought to light. My hope is that it brings comfort and direction to all of us as we try to navigate our way through this complex universe.

I would also like to thank those friends and colleagues who have provided encouragement throughout this project. I want to acknowledge Jeff Danelek for his input and for his friendship. To my wife, thank you for your continual love and support. And to the guides who shared these insights, I feel honored to have been a part of such a profound experience.

# Contents

# Introduction

I don't talk to dead people. I don't see ghosts, and I don't claim to be anything more than the recorder of the amazing things I witness every day. But there is so much wisdom all around us, wisdom that comes from guides, angels, spirits, and other forms of energy. And my job is simply to help *others* communicate with their guides and record the information that *they* are given. I practice a variation of a modality called alchemical hypnotherapy.

One of the most powerful tools of an alchemical hypnotherapist is asking for a client to bring in their guides to assist in helping them navigate their way through life. I don't bring in these otherworldly advisors; the client does. I have no control over who they bring in, whether it is an angel, an animal totem, a ball of energy, a spirit guide, a saint, or even Jesus Christ. I ask questions of these guides, but it is *always* the client who answers the questions by first listening to the source and then relaying information *they* are given.

After 13 years of utilizing this process, one would expect that the guidance and information would always be moving in different directions and relevant only to the specific individual client and their personal journey, but that isn't the case. Although each piece of wisdom might be customized and carefully worded for that individual, there are universal themes that occur again and again, regardless of the bringer of the wisdom. In a sense, it is as if the information is coming from one voice.

So, what are we being told? What do the guides want us to know? And what if I started asking questions about life, death, the afterlife, karma, parallel planes, healing, and why we exist on this planet? That is exactly what unfolded, and this is a compilation of what I have recorded during those hypnotherapy sessions. If there wasn't a remarkable consistency in the answers, there would be no basis for this book, but how could it be that the same answers come forth regardless whether the client was talking to an angel, an animal totem, a ball of energy, a spirit guide, a saint, or even Jesus Christ? How could it be that the same information was given regardless of whether the client was a Christian, a Jew, an atheist, or one who describes themselves as metaphysical? And how could it be that many of those answers challenge the spiritual foundations that we have come to accept?

In this book, I've tried to capture the messages we are being given. Each chapter contains transcripts of dialogues that have taken place in actual sessions, so the reader can seek out the wisdom that might help them move forward in their own quest for knowledge and enlightenment.

Other writers have written books in which they channeled information from the spiritual realm, and although some of those books are intriguing, the perspectives they present could potentially be colored by the personal biases of the authors. Those books are derived from a single source of information. This book is different because it is a compilation from many sources. I am not the one channeling information, and the purpose of this work is *not* to tell you how to think or what to believe. My role was to be the objective reporter and record the communications given to clients as they conversed with their own personal guides. What I do share is my journey: I started out with my own ideas and beliefs, only to have many of those turned upside down during this process.

Along the way, there were many surprises. For example, I never thought the information from the guides would be so forthcoming. It seemed like no topic was off the table. The bigger issue was the frustration expressed by the guides when they tried to explain concepts that were impossible to describe with our limited human vocabulary.

# Why Hypnosis

Hypnosis is a therapeutic modality that helps people directly access the subconscious mind. Most of the time, we operate within the constraints of our conscious or critical minds—two interchangeable descriptions for the thinking mind—which is where we do our cognitive functions such as reasoning, analysis, and logic. The subconscious mind is the part of us that holds our memories, experiences, and the source or roots of all of the issues and lessons we face in our lifetime. It is in the subconscious realm where we have a connection to the spiritual world. It provides access to communicate with our inner spirit or soul, and it allows us to tap into the reason we are here and what we are here to learn. It is the window to higher knowledge. Throughout history, the great spiritual leaders and teachers have gone into prayer or meditation to enter a subconscious trance state in order to access the guidance they needed to help humankind. Only the subconscious mind can open a window to communications and wisdom from other dimensions, not the critical mind.

Through the use of hypnosis, the subconscious is accessible to everyone, and by using that modality in this context, participants were able to communicate with their guides, something that would not have been possible in a normal conscious state. Without the use of hypnosis or some kind of trance state, clients in this project would have simply responded to these questions with answers from their critical minds. In other words, it would have been nothing more than a survey of opinions. Hypnosis was the means by which the guides were able to convey information or wisdom from another realm.

There is a great deal of misinformation about hypnosis due to unfamiliarity and misconceptions. Hypnotherapy is quickly becoming accepted as a means by which you can do life-changing work. Traditionally, it was widely used for stress reduction, fears and phobias, weight management, and smoking cessation. As the practice of hypnotherapy has evolved, it has become a popular modality for working with infertility, relationship issues, pain management, insomnia, birthing, healing, and much more.

The truth about hypnosis is:

❧ The client is *always* in control during the process.

❧ It is not a form of mind control. A hypnotist cannot make you rob banks and bring the money back to them.

❧ There is no sleeping in hypnosis. Yes, in the movies, usually someone resembling a mad scientist will say "Go to sleep" in order to induce a trance, but if you've ever tried talking to someone who is asleep, you know from experience, that doesn't work. People who are asleep, if they talk at all, typically speak in nonsensical ramblings.

❧ In hypnosis, people remember and are aware of everything that goes on during their sessions.

❧ Hypnosis is not a form of truth serum in which you give away your deepest, darkest secrets.

And if any of the misconceptions about hypnosis were true, it would be illegal.

Hypnosis is similar to meditation or experiencing a deep prayer state. The participant is *always* aware and in control in all three of those modalities.

The most important use of hypnotherapy is accessing information that is holding people back from being successful in their lives. Commonly, the roots or sources of our fears, anxieties, anger, and other issues can be uncovered and processed through this modality. It can also be an amazing conduit for connecting with spiritual wisdom and uncovering the answers we all seek as we try to navigate our way on this planet.

# What Is Alchemical Hypnosis?

The origins of alchemy go back thousands of years. Generally, when people think of alchemy, they think of the process of transmuting metals into gold, but in relation to personal growth, the term became a metaphor to describe the process of changing the nature or spirit of an individual in a positive way. Initially, chemicals, elixirs, potions, and even metals were used to assist in personal transformations, and the objective of this transmutation process was to heal from diseases, difficulties, ailments, and evils. Some people believed that through alchemy one could experience rejuvenation and perhaps even achieve immortality. With time, the practice of alchemy shifted and became more focused on the spiritual and mystical. In the 1940s, Carl Jung adapted the process into his psychoanalytic methods, working with archetypes and inner guides.

In contemporary alchemical hypnotherapy, clients often work with various inner guides. For example, an individual who lacks self-esteem might, during their session, bring in various parts of themselves including their inner child, their inner judge, their rebellious self, and their neglected self. Then, with the assistance of the hypnotist, there might be discussions and mediation between those "parts" in order to release some of the old patterns and beliefs that could then be replaced by a new, more positive dynamic.

In this project, the emphasis was on external guides instead of inner guides. Either of those resources can be used in alchemical hypnotherapy as the goal is the same: to take the base metal, or person who is struggling, and assist them in turning themselves and their lives into a more golden existence.

# The Participants

The participants included both male and female clients of various races who ranged in age from 15 to those in their early 70s. The goal was to represent people from a broad spectrum of spiritual or religious beliefs, as well as from various age groups and genders. The majority of the participants grew up in families that had practiced one of the traditional religions. Many of those religions included various forms of Christianity. When asked about their upbringing, clients responded with everything from Southern Baptist and Catholicism to Episcopalian and Judaism. Some of those participants were still involved with those religions, whereas others had either gone on to pursue spirituality on their own or had changed to a different religion through the years. Many participants were uncertain about their spirituality and entered this process unsure if there was a God or angels or anything beyond our existence here on Earth. Some participants only believed in "Earth energy" and were okay communicating with totems or animal spirits, but didn't necessarily believe that there was a God.

Here is a rough breakdown of what clients had said, prior to the beginning of their session, when I asked their *conscious minds* about their spiritual beliefs. It is important to note that this was the response in the waking state where they were using their critical minds and *not* their response during hypnosis.

| | |
|---|---|
| 30% | Are strongly connected to a religion (most often Christian-based). |
| 25% | Refer to themselves as "spiritual but not religious." |
| 20% | Are unsure about spiritually and don't know what to believe. |
| 13% | Don't believe in God or spirituality at all. |
| 12% | Feel a strong connection to the Earth energy, but aren't sure about God. |

Perhaps the most interesting observation in those numbers is that there is a fair amount of uncertainty in the overall population when it comes to religion and spirituality.

In the process of conducting these sessions and asking about the nature of God, religion, and spirituality, I reminded each participant that they were to always share the perspectives of their guides even though it might differ from their personal beliefs. That was a condition that each individual had to honor in order to participate. I believe the clients did respect that commitment because there were many times, after the sessions, that individuals told me that they disagreed with or were quite surprised by the information they received.

I owe much gratitude to the many volunteers who participated in this project. This was truly a collaborative effort. In a sense, we were all serving as vehicles through which this information was conveyed, and it all came together as a collection of what the *guides* want us to know, expressed by them, sharing *their* incredible wisdom and insights.

# Confidentiality

As a practitioner, I have the utmost respect for confidentiality, and I assured each subject that their confidentiality would be honored and each would be given a fictitious name. It is also my legal obligation to protect every client's identity. Although it might have been interesting for me to provide background information such as "John is a 43-year-old computer programmer who grew up in a strict Catholic household and is a staunch Republican," that information might be enough to breach confidentiality. Unless the background information was relevant to the response, all identifying material about each client has been withheld.

As I worked on this project, it was as if the identifying information about each client became immaterial. The client acted primarily as a medium or vehicle through which the messages were conveyed, so the personal identity of the client really became irrelevant. I don't mean that those people were not important, because they were vitally important, but their participation was more like a channel and not the origin of the information. I liken it to watching a major presidential speech on television: it doesn't matter what channel you tune into, the message is the same, and in this dynamic, the primary focus was on the message.

## The Accuracy of the Responses

Skeptics might try to argue that these are simply the opinions of the participants and not really deeper communication with another realm. However, if 50 people were gathered and asked a question such as "What happens when you die" while they were in the conscious state, there would be myriad answers, discussions, and disagreements. Ten of those people might say you go to heaven. Ten might believe in reincarnation. Ten might suggest that you become part of a spiritual realm. Ten might say that you simply decay and go back into the earth. And, at least 10 would probably come back and say, "I don't know." But when I asked that same question to people in alchemical hypnosis—regardless of whether the response came from an angel, a spirit guide, a deceased ancestor, a religious leader, or even God Himself—the answers showed an amazing degree of consistency. When 50 people give the exact same answer to that question, and in many cases that answer conflicts with their personal beliefs, this suggests that these answers were not biased opinions, nor were they coming from the conscious mind.

As the interviewer, it was important for me not to "lead" the client in a way that would influence their answers. I had to make sure I avoided questions that reflected a bias or expectation. For example, a question such as "What happens when you die?" is not a leading question because the answer can go in a variety of directions. An example of a leading question would be "What is it like in heaven?" That question implies that there is a heaven and that when we die we, in fact, go to heaven.

In many cases, I do recap or rephrase responses in order to clarify answers because, often, the replies weren't entirely clear or the reply might be making reference to something that was mentioned earlier in the session. On many occasions, it was necessary and more interesting to pursue a reply with follow-up questions and that is why the interviews are presented in dialogue form.

It is important to note that many of the answers were not grammatically correct. Others didn't have agreement with tense or structure. Sometimes words were included that were in a form that would be considered improper usage. I didn't edit those. It was critical to capture the exact messages from the guides the way they were expressed to me. If I had made changes and cleaned up tense, verb/subject agreement, and made everything into complete sentences, the accuracy and authenticity would have been lost. The objective was to capture this information exactly as it was communicated from the guides. During this process, it was interesting to observe clients who are very articulate, well-spoken individuals in everyday life, sometimes speak in fragments, in run-on sentences, and in disregard for agreement in tenses and subject matter when they relayed the communications they received.

Additionally, there are very few ellipses contained in these conversations. An ellipsis indicates that something has been removed or omitted from the conversation. It would have been disingenuous to alter or doctor the messages rather than do my best to present them as they were shared with me.

Although some of these questions, such as "What happens when you die?" are queries everyone has pondered and can answer fairly quickly—even if they often say they don't know—many of the questions concerned subjects that the clients in all likelihood hadn't considered. When asked to discuss a topic such as parallel planes, most people are not prepared and don't have an answer at the ready. Yet, none of the respondents said, "I don't know." Instead, each one listened to their guides and then immediately gave answers that often went far beyond anything that most conscious minds could ever envision.

Finally, although input from people who specialize in the area of spirituality can often be insightful, I wanted to honor the wisdom of the guides by presenting this information in its purist form by purposefully excluding commentary or opinions of those who are considered experts in this field. My strategy was to discuss and analyze each piece of information on its own merits rather than tainting the messages with theories and ideas the scholars and theologians have pieced together through time. The insertion of human-based perspectives would have increased the likelihood of corrupting or misrepresenting the true intent of the communications, and it would have altered the purpose of this book, which was to focus on the wisdom of the guides, rather than presenting opinions that have been influenced by human logic and man-made belief systems.

## What I Did and Didn't Expect

The inspiration for this book came out of 13 years of working with hypnotherapy clients. In a session of alchemical hypnosis, it was not unusual to work with a guide to help the client gain perspective. By bringing in a guide, the client could get an objective opinion about the issue they were addressing. For example, a client who felt guilty about something they had done earlier in life might be reassured by their guardian angel that God forgave them and it would be okay for them to let go of that guilt.

But what about the clients who didn't believe in angels? If alchemical hypnosis was appropriate to the issue we were addressing in the session, I would ask the client if they would feel comfortable inviting in some sort of guide to help them on their journey. In many of those cases, they would end up working with an animal or a spirit guide or even their higher self. I would always let them choose, and on many occasions, we would simply extend an open invitation and see who would appear.

With time, I discovered that we have an abundance of help on the other side, and these guides seem to be extremely supportive and wanting to assist in any way they can. People can call in angels or totems, a deceased ancestor, or a religious figure such as Jesus, or even talk directly to God or the Universe. Even clients who are unsure about religion or their spirituality seem to be able to easily access a guide to help them.

Naturally, I expected a broad spectrum of answers to these inquiries. I thought the angel would have a different answer from the animal totem, and the animal totem would have a different answer from an ancestor who, in turn, would have a different answer from a master guide, and so on. I also suspected that the answer from the Christian would markedly differ from that of the metaphysical client, which would differ from the individual who had no spiritual beliefs at all. But that wasn't the case. Regardless of the guide and regardless of the personal beliefs of the client, there were some strikingly similar elements to these communications, and it was quite common for the answers to conflict with what one would have expected the client or the guide to say. For example, a conservative Christian, working with an angel as their guide, might surprise me by talking about how we have many lives and can experience parallel planes of existence. And there were several occasions where the guides of agnostic or atheistic clients would freely talk about Divine energy.

With time, there were elements of consistency and thematic revelations that caught my attention. In some cases, it almost felt like my clients were secretly comparing notes and answers before their sessions because it felt like the information was coming from one voice. Naturally, they weren't doing that, so I thought it would be fascinating to see if I asked the same set of questions to a wide variety of people—and a wide variety of guides—would that same uniformity exist?

Instead of asking questions specific to my client's situations, with each client's permission, I started asking for information about the spiritual realm. After all, humankind has spent thousands of years contemplating the nature of the Universe, the mysteries around life and death, and the nature of our existence. What if we could unlock some of those secrets?

I did have a concern when I opened this work up to those universal topics. The question I had was how much information the guides would be willing to share. Sometimes, in sessions I had conducted in the past, the communication was limited. Although those guides were always ready to help a client with an issue such as forgiveness, if I followed up with a question such as "What happens when we die?" sometimes very little information would come forth. The guide might look at them in a loving way, but not answer the question. I suspected that this lack of response would occur when it appeared that the question was something the client was not ready to know or something they would need to discover as they accumulated more years of life experience.

So, when I conducted the sessions for the book, I made it clear to all of the guides that I intended to ask tough questions. In a different context there might not have been as much free-flowing information, but this project was for those individuals who really needed those answers to help them on their life journey. I would start the communication by saying: "These answers are for the people who need guidance in their lives. This is for people who are lost or anxious or fearful. This is for people who want a better understanding about life and death and what happens when we die. This is for people who are seeking peace in their lives and people who are looking for a spiritual path that feels authentic and nurtures them." Essentially, I was saying to the guides: "This isn't a time to withhold information; let's help as many people as we can."

The guides responded in an amazing way. Although there were many times where they were hampered by the lack of English vocabulary needed to explain their concepts, the guides were present and would try to answer every question I posed. During the project, I was continually moved by their amazing dedication and desire to help. There was also a very tangible loving presence during the sessions. I could feel it as the interviewer, and the clients were often touched by the overwhelming love and support.

I didn't know that this would turn out to be such a profound experience for my clients. Many reported that the connection they experienced was truly amazing. I would try to thank them for helping me out and they would want to correct me and say "No, thank you," because the process was so rich for them.

Although there were benefits for the clients, it was also an important process in my evolution. I never expected that this would become a personal journey of discovery. Sometimes, during a session, the guides would have messages specifically for me. One guide, through a female client, spoke of this directly to me:

> *Jim, this is not about other people. This is about you. This is about your questions, and people will be exceedingly interested in the answers to your questions, but they're your questions and this is your journey, and so the more you try to figure this out for other people, the less power it will have. The more you try to figure this out from the very personal place, ask the questions you want to ask, not the questions you think other people want to ask, you will answer the important questions. This has to be personal. It can't be impersonal. It can't be for someone else. In being selfish, you end up being selfless.*

And, indeed, with each interview, I wanted to know more. I wanted to know intricate details about our journey. I became fascinated by the process and found myself looking inward to see how this information related directly to my life experiences. I even asked a few questions specific to my life, with the newfound assurance that the answers would be universal and help everyone.

Perhaps the biggest surprise was in the answers themselves. In my studies of spirituality, I had expectations about how each question would be answered. Time and time again, I was surprised. Some of these answers might challenge the beliefs you have, but the purpose of this project was to provide guidance for all of us who are struggling to make sense of this journey of life. I hope this book provides comfort, direction, and enlightenment to everyone so that they may feel a sense of inner peace as we all try to navigate our way through life on this planet.

# Who Are Our Guides?

At the beginning of each session, I had clients imagine that they were going to a very sacred, spiritual place. This progression would take about 15 minutes and part of that process was to help each individual gently transition into a lighter, more peaceful state in which they were open and accepting of whomever came forward to work with them. It is important to reiterate that the choice of the guide was completely up to the client and never based on my input or opinion.

On many occasions, clients would bring in more than one guide. An example of this was Chris. During his session, Chris worked with a rainbow, a sphere of light, a Native American shaman, and Source energy.

What kind of guides appeared during these sessions? Here is a breakdown and description of the different types of guides *chosen by the clients* in this research.

**Spirit guides:** 22 percent of the sessions.

Spirit guides tend to appear in human form. For example, a spirit guide might have the look of a Native American Indian or an elderly sage who appears to be from another time and place.

A common belief is that we each have a spirit guide who is assigned to us throughout our entire life, but spirit guides can also be with us on a temporary basis during which they help us with a specific lesson or challenge and then move on.

**Totems/animal guides:** 21 percent of the sessions.

Totems are animals that serve as guides to people. They can also be referred to as spirit animals or power animals. These can be wild animals or even faithful pets that have made their transition.

**Angels:** 16 percent of the sessions.

Angels and archangels typically emanate a beautiful radiant light and are considered to be an intermediary between humans and the Divine. When visited by an angel, most people report that the energy is luminous, but rarely are they able to see definitive facial features of an angel.

**Light or energy:** 12 percent of the sessions.

This may actually be an expression of Source, but clients who aren't sure they believe in God will sometimes be guided by a light, a ball of energy, a color, or an energy field. Despite the lack of a tangible physical form, these guides can still communicate either verbally or telepathically.

**A master guide or advanced spiritual teacher:** 8 percent of the sessions.

A master guide differs from a spirit guide in that they operate on a much higher level. In other words, these guides are very highly evolved. They might concurrently work with many people and can also work to help heal the energy and consciousness of the planet. Master guides can sometimes appear in human form, but masters can also have a shape that is not of this world.

**Source or God:** 8 percent of the sessions.

When a client accesses Source or God, it is usually in the form of a voice, a light, or a vibration of energy. There never seems to be a physical embodiment or physical form when an individual works with Source.

**Jesus:** 7 percent of the sessions.

Because of their religious leanings, for some individuals, Jesus feels very safe; however, it is surprising how often Jesus will appear with clients who don't consider themselves to be religious. In some situations, Jesus could also fall into the category of a very evolved master guide.

**Alien:** 4 percent of the sessions.

Aliens are simply spiritual beings that are not in human form.

It is best to disregard the science fiction imagery of aliens and, instead, think of these benevolent beings as simply having a non-human appearance.

**Ancestors:** 2 percent of the sessions.

An ancestor will typically be a relative who has passed on, but was strongly connected to the client during their lifetime.

For example, a loving grandfather or grandmother might appear and want to help with guidance. On rare occasions, an ancestor can be from many generations prior to the birth of the client.

One caution with ancestors is that sometimes a deceased relative who was a negative energy during their time on Earth may still have that negativity if they haven't done their work. In those situations, the advice may not be for the client's highest good and it is best to call in another guide. In these sessions, an ancestor was only allowed to participate if there were clear indications that the ancestor was an evolved being of love and light.

There were other guides that emerged in this process that didn't perfectly fit into these groupings, but I tried to place those exceptions as appropriately as possible. For example, the rainbow Chris described became part of the "light or energy" classification.

There can also be some overlap in these categories. For example, someone talking to a ball of light might have been communicating with a spirit guide or possibly conversing with Source. The message was far more relevant than the form or shape of the communicating entity, as that was the primary focus of this work.

Individuals were sometimes surprised by who came forward to work with them. For instance, someone who resonated with angels might have been greeted by an animal totem, such as a wolf or a panther. Someone who believed in spirit guides might have found that it was Jesus who spent time with them.

Sometimes those surprises were greater than others. One woman who was raised in a household that was a very strict Christian environment—and had gone on to reject all connections to formal religion—demonstrated how the process could sometimes take an unexpected turn. This is how Maryanne's session unfolded when I asked her about her guide:

JS: Who comes forward to work with you today?

Maryanne: I heard someone say that they were here, but they haven't identified themselves yet.

JS: Just tune in and ask if they're willing to work with us today.

Maryanne: They said yes, and I'd know who they were in a while.

I waited until the end of the session before I brought up the subject again. I was curious to know the identity of the guide who was working with Maryanne, so I asked again.

JS: Before we wrap up, can you [the guide] identify yourself so we can express gratitude to who's been helping us today?

During some sessions, there would be times where the client and the guide had differing opinions or, in some cases, a little bit of a disconnect. In this response, the guide actually mentions Maryanne's resistance.

Maryanne: She's been resisting this identity all day. I told her earlier and she said no, no, no, that's not it.

After a long pause, the answer came.

Maryanne: It's Jesus. But she says no. She's in big denial about that whole Jesus thing.

JS: Because of her exposure to religious dogma?

Maryanne: Yes. Yes, and she experienced it firsthand, so she fights it tooth and nail, but here I am.

Some people might view direct discussions with Source or God or Jesus as being somehow blasphemous or not appropriate, but time and time again in these sessions, the guides encouraged us to connect or communicate with them on a more regular basis. It became very clear; they want a connection with us.

Sometimes there were commonalities, especially in appearance, to the guides who met with the clients. There were some master guides who had the form of a grasshopper or cricket. This is how one of the clients described this type of master guide:

Sonya: This is really weird. There's another being in the room, and it looks like a grasshopper kind of. It's very white, but it has kind of a grasshopper face with swirly antennas. I don't know what that thing is.

JS: Are you okay with this guide being there?

Sonya: Yeah. He seems very serious, not scary, very knowledgeable. That was the first thing I saw [when she was asked to invite a guide to come forth], but I didn't really want to talk to that one. So there's that guy, there's the teacher guy, and then there's what I'm thinking is an angel that's really pretty white.

Again, as I mentioned earlier with Chris, it wasn't uncommon for multiple guides to participate in the sessions.

On rare occasions, clients observed what they called aliens. For clarification, the word *alien* has taken on a very different connotation as a result of the portrayal they have received in the movies and on television. In this context, aliens can be beings from other planets or galaxies or they can simply be life forms that are different from humans. This is how aliens were described in one of the sessions in which the client was accompanied by a guide who would take her on journeys to actually see or get visions of the answers: "In this vision, they [the aliens] are not really living on the planet. They're with a star or something, and they know about us. And they are just kind of there. They don't talk. They're telepathic, and they don't seem very personable as compared to humans. But they're not really scary like I thought aliens would be. They're just really smart."

Regardless of what guides came forward, the environment always felt safe and supportive. One client, who expressed some frustration in attempting to describe being in the presence of the guides, put it this way: "It feels very supportive, like being held. The energy of it is like being held. The reason I say that is because there is no judgment. That doesn't quite say enough, but that's all I have."

## The Process

Each hypnosis session began with what is called an induction. An induction is the process by which a client gently goes into hypnosis. After the client had entered hypnosis, I would lead them on a journey to a very sacred place. I let them know that this sacred place was not affiliated with a specific religion, belief system, or teaching. It was simply a place where they could be open to receiving information from whatever beings or energies emerged. I wanted each client to feel free to communicate with whomever they felt comfortable. It was important for everyone to know that there was no judgment around this, and whatever guide materialized was perfectly fine.

It wasn't uncommon for the client to be surprised by who came forward to share. In other words, prior to the beginning of the process, the client might have expected to speak to their guardian angel, but when they reached that sacred place, it might have been a spirit guide or animal that came forth to speak with them.

About one third of the clients channeled the communication. Channeling is where the being, entity, or energy speaks directly through the client. This is a fascinating process because the individual who is channeling often has a dramatic change in intonation, inflection, vocabulary choices, pacing, and delivery. It is almost as if the person channeling becomes a completely different personality. Prior to the session, they might average 100 spoken words per minute. During the session, they might speak six words per minute with an accent and a completely different cadence. It is important to note that none of these clients had ever channeled or had any idea that they had that potential.

The difference between an individual who channels and one who doesn't is that when a person channels, it is as if the energy speaks directly through them, which is why there are changes in intonation, phrasing, and inflection. The non-channeling clients were still getting their information from the guides, but the delivery was different because they would first listen to the guide's answer and then relay that answer to me with their normal voice and inflection. In one case, the guide speaks *through* the client and in the other, it is a conversation between the guide and the client. In my observations, I didn't feel that one method was more powerful or accurate than the other; I was more interested in the message than the delivery.

Each time I asked a question, the non-channeling clients would usually pause in order to wait for the communicating energy to respond. Sometimes they would listen for a minute or more, to get all the information, and then they would relay the answer that was told to them. In some cases, clients shared with me that they wanted to give their own personal answer to one of the questions, but their guides reminded them to step back and instead let the answer come from the source. In fact, it wasn't uncommon for individuals, after the work was done, to tell me that they disagreed with an answer that was given during the session, but honored their agreement to simply relay the information without expressing any personal bias.

Once a client experienced the powerful energy and connection of that very spiritual, sacred place that I used for the purpose of this project, many conveyed a feeling of euphoria. Occasionally, a client would feel a sense of sadness when I asked them to come back to the present time and, once again, become grounded in their body. One of the subjects described her experience during that session in a way that captured the sentiments relayed to me by many of the participants:

> *While I have experienced profound moments of the Divine, my time with you remains a significant benchmark on my soul's eternal journey. I was the Light, and the Light was me. There was no separation from this Light. Words simply fail to express that feeling of Oneness.*

After I worked with a few clients and heard comments like this, I could see that there was something incredibly profound occurring in these sessions. Perhaps this process allowed these clients to truly feel and briefly exist at an elevated vibration where they felt completely connected to Source energy. Maybe it was similar to the incredible sense of warmth, comfort, and unconditional love that people report when undergoing near-death experiences. I can't say for sure, but these extraordinary responses gave me inspiration and let me know that something about this work was very important.

## Chapter 1

# What Is the True Nature of the Divine?

My introduction to spirituality in my early life was our family's tenuous connection with the Catholic religion. We didn't go to church every Sunday. Our attendance at mass and catechism was sporadic at best, but it was my initiation to religion and spirituality. I was intrigued by the ritual, the traditions within the church, and the stories of the Bible. Something about having a deeper connection to God innately felt right to me.

Unfortunately, most of the emphasis in my experience with Catholicism wasn't on the ceremonies or rituals or storytelling, it was much more about the dogma. On numerous occasions, we were told that if we were bad, we were going to go to hell. The idea of heaven was plausible, but even at an early age, I didn't buy into the idea of hell. It sounded to me as if it was no more than a way to scare young boys and girls into behaving.

As a boy, I would go to church with my father and my brother. My father would not take communion. He always acted as if he wasn't allowed to participate in that sacrament. I remember how that troubled me. I was taught to honor and respect my elders, and here was this man I looked up to who wasn't okay in the eyes of the church. On some level there was an element of guilt—it felt truly palpable on those Sundays when I was there with him—and an element of punishment and non-forgiveness that were all part of that experience.

Because such things were never spoken about at that time, it wasn't until later that I understood the reality of the situation. I learned that the issue was that my father and mother had divorced when I was quite young, and he had remarried without ever having the first marriage annulled. Divorce and remarriage without annulment was a sin in the eyes of the Catholic Church and that made him unworthy. By association, when going to church with my father, it felt like all of us were outsiders.

As I grew older, I always wanted a connection with Spirit. I was torn because I didn't find resonance with traditional religions. I could see the importance of formal religion for many people: it gave them a sense of community, a sense of structure, and a connection to the Divine. But I felt like I didn't fit into that structure. I felt a strong sense of connection with God or the Divine or the Great Spirit or whatever word was used to describe that energy, but there never seemed to be a good fit for me when it came to organized religion.

Years later, as I worked in my practice, I found a lot of people in my same predicament: searching for some type of spiritual connection, but not comfortable with traditional religions. The reason I know this is because in alchemical hypnosis work, we often work with guides, and before the beginning of a session, I would always ask clients about their spirituality. That was the safest route so that I didn't end up saying things that were incongruent with that client's belief system. For example, some people are okay with words like

*Universe* or *energy*, but are not comfortable referring to that energy as God. Some might be okay with angels, but feel spirit guides are too metaphysical. Some don't believe in spirituality at all and don't want to do work in that realm. I didn't bring up these conversations to try to influence or change a client's belief system; I simply didn't want to offend anyone by saying something that might conflict with their principles or conviction. So, I always found it best, before beginning any of our work together, to get a clear understanding of their spirituality, or in some cases, an absence of spirituality.

# Three Concerns With the First Question

In addressing this first question, an inquiry about the true nature or essence of the Divine, I had three areas of concern. In some ways, the answers to this question would either validate or invalidate whether I was actually communicating with the guides or whether the responses, on some level, were merely coming from the conscious minds of the participants.

1. That was the first concern: what if the answers to this question turned out to be no more than a conscious mind expression of the beliefs of the clients? In an earlier section of this book, called "The Participants," I outlined a breakdown of what people had told me, prior to our hypnosis sessions, about what they believe in terms of religion and spirituality. About half of the respondents, though expressing a few vague notions about their leanings, could best be described as unsure about what they believe. When I asked questions about God, religion, and spirituality in these conscious discussions, many would preface their answers with "I don't know," "That's a good question," or "I'm not really sure."

   What if the answers that were supposed to be from the guides were identical to the pre-session responses that came from the clients during their intake interviews? What if the answers from the guides expressed that same degree of uncertainty? By opening the guided wisdom sessions with a question about the nature of the Divine, it provided an opportunity to see if the responses were truly coming from the clients or from the guides. If the subjects were expressing their personal opinions, then the answers would break down into the same percentages reflected by the data I had collected in pre-session interviews. If the answers significantly deviated from the pre-session statistics, then that would suggest that the guides were the source of the information.

2. The second concern was if the participants might respond with answers that mirrored what they had been taught early in life when many were exposed to traditional religion. The subconscious mind can be a vehicle for accessing past memories and experiences, and because most of us were exposed to organized religion at an early age, there was a possibility that the respondents would simply regress back in time and provide information that replicated their exposure to those early doctrines. However, when clients go back in time, they can usually be objective about their past experiences. If the answers strongly reflected traditional religious ideologies, the concern would be that somehow those old beliefs were coming back to the surface.

3. There was yet another possible outcome, and third concern, that I considered. This third concern was if the guides associated with a specific religion would only respond in a way that was congruent with that faith. For example, what if Jesus, acting as a guide for a client, would only espouse Christian ideology even if the client didn't embrace that belief system? And would Buddha only adhere to Buddhism? I didn't feel that this was likely because that had never been the case in sessions conducted prior to this research, but it was a possibility.

In short, I was aware that there were potential outcomes connected to this specific question—more than any of the others—that would indicate whether the replies were simply human responses or we were accessing another realm and genuinely capturing the wisdom of the guides.

Fortunately, none of those concerns proved to be an issue: the answers *did not* fall into any of those worrisome scenarios. The doubt and uncertainty that clients expressed in pre-session interviews were not present with the guides. Early religious programming was not reflected in the replies, and guides associated with religions—such as Jesus—freely expressed ideas that often deviated from the corresponding belief system associated with that figure. Despite the wide diversity of backgrounds of the participants, the responses to this question had a surprisingly strong thematic consistency. The answers were not at all what I expected. In fact, the insights from this first inquiry represented the beginning of a journey into rethinking much of the programming we have come to accept about religion and spirituality.

❧

To begin the interview process of each session, I would start by asking the client to invite their guide(s) to come in, and then I would ask the guides to identify themselves. Once that connection was established, the first question was always an inquiry about the essence or nature of the Divine. I tried to phrase it in such a way that was open to a variety of responses, such as how I have expressed it in the following:

> JS: Is there such a thing as God or Divine or Universe or whatever description you want to use, and if so, what is the essence or nature of the Divine?

I should mention that I didn't distinguish between the various terms used to describe the Divine. It could be Source, Creator, Energy, Divine, Spirit, God, Universe, or a number of other descriptors. I would often use those words interchangeably and try to give the guide several choices so they could choose one or they could say that none of the above exists. If the response was affirmative and utilized one of those terms, I would try to echo whichever term was spoken by that individual during the remainder of the interview.

In this book, I made a concerted effort to include those conversations that captured or represented the views expressed in the majority of the responses. It is important to remember that even though I use fictitious client names in the dialogue portions of this book, the clients are relaying answers that come from their guides and *not* responding with their own beliefs. In cases where an individual might have shared how they feel or what they personally believe— and not echoing the information from their guides—I have tried to make that clear in the text.

So, what is the nature or essence of the Divine? The first excerpt comes from a client I call Megan, working with a master guide, and I chose to start with this dialogue because her response was very typical of the many answers to this question.

JS: Is there such a thing as God or Source or Creator? And if so, what is the nature or essence of that entity?

Megan: It's all around. It's everywhere. It's the source of all things. A lot of people think that it's a being of some kind, but it's sort of a source of energy, an innateness in everything.

JS: So this image that we've created of the man with a white beard in the clouds, that's not it?

Megan: No.

JS: You used the word *energy*. Is that a good word to describe it?

Megan: Yes, that's a good word.

JS: And you said "all around us," can you talk about that?

Megan: Well, it's in everything, so it's all around you, all around us, in the things that get created that are used by people. That's the God energy. That comes from the God energy. The people around us are created from the God energy.

JS: So that energy is in all people, all plants, animals, all things, is that right?

Megan: Yeah.

JS: Is the source or the nature of that energy a loving, forgiving kind of energy? Some people believe that Divine energy is punishing and vengeful. What is its true nature?

Megan: It's allowing, forgiving, accepting, loving.

JS: Not punishing?

Megan: No.

That dialogue, in some ways, might be a preview of some of the conversations to come in this chapter. First, the Divine is described as an energy and not a being or entity or a man in the clouds waiting to pass judgment. That energy is present in all things, and it is portrayed as loving and forgiving, not punishing.

I included those last questions because so many individuals have learned to associate shame, guilt, and an element of punishment with the Divine. One of the guides summed up what dozens of sessions had come to bare when I asked about shame, guilt, non-forgiveness, and punishment: "That is human. Humans made that up." That same guide went on to remind us about the true essence of God's energy: "It's just love."

Lia's guide, a being of light, expressed her reply a little differently, but the information was consistent. The idea that there is no separation between man and the Divine was reinforced in this response.

JS: Is there a God or Divine or Universe or whatever description you want to use, and if so, what is the essence or nature of the Divine?

Lia: It is all there is.

JS: What does that mean?

Lia: There is this profound pulse of energy, and from that is all this light and love, and this is where everything comes from. And it is really all we are.

JS: What is the connection between people and this Divine energy?

Lia: It is us, and we are this energy. There is no separation.

JS: This God energy is in every one of us, is that what you're saying?

Lia: Yes, it is in everything. It is in the space between everything.

Once again, the Divine was described as energy, and, again, the message is that there is no separation between Divine energy and the energy inside each of us. Some religions claim that there is a separation between man and God. There was *never* a sense of that in these responses. It was quite the opposite. Time and time again, the message was that Divine energy is in all of us.

Many of the subjects received their answers by being shown scenes or actually experiencing moments or visions that gave them the answers to the questions. This was the case with Nicole. Her guide, a tiger, was continually allowing her to have experiential understandings.

JS: If God exists, what is the true essence of God?

Nicole: Breath and warmth. There is a fire, a creation. I'm seeing a horizon and light hitting the horizon, and at the same time I'm feeling a warmth in my belly, and it's telling me that it's the same experience. It's inseparable. There's a joy, a sense of open bliss.

JS: You mentioned a connection. You said I see it, I feel it inside of me. Can you talk about that?

Nicole: Yes, there is a familiarity, a similarity. For me, right now it's showing me a plane and then the sunlight hitting the plane, and when the sunlight and the plane blend, it becomes the same color and the same light. It's this yellowish warm color and light, and I can feel that inside also.

JS: You described this as bliss. Are you saying that this energy is a positive energy?

Nicole: It's loving and warm and it's open. It's not catching on anything. It doesn't have boundary to it.

JS: You said that it's inside you. When you say no boundary, do we all have this?

Nicole: Yeah. And it's connected to the earth and sky and sun. It doesn't feel separate, but within my body, within the 3-D or physical, it feels separate, but it isn't. It's like the blending of the sky and the sun.

JS: Are you saying that this spirit energy is in all of us?

Nicole: Um-hm.

JS: What about those of us that have heard that God is punishing and vengeful?

Nicole [laughing]: Why? Why would that be? There's a mistake in that thinking. First of all, they're showing me this [about] personification: There's no person of God. It's not a person. People have feelings like that.

JS: So it's more like an energy field, not like the way we depict God here as a human?

Nicole: There's no person, no face. It's faceless. It's big, *big* energy. It doesn't look like a human, that's for sure [laughing]. That's silly thinking.

Nicole's guides didn't support the visual representations humans have created through the years depicting God as a physical entity or human being. The repeated message in these communications was that Divine energy is in all humans, and it is *an* energy, not, as it has been depicted for centuries, some sort of being or entity or a man with a white beard sitting in the clouds. The other conviction that was quickly becoming debunked was the idea that God and man are separate entities. Nicole's tiger described the dynamic as having "no boundaries." The responses from the guides continually affirmed that there was no separation; God is not a separate energy, and God energy is in all of us. For Nicole, she said being in a three-dimensional human body might make us feel we are separate from the Divine, but she went on to say that this wasn't true.

It wasn't uncommon for the guides to show my clients various scenes in order to allow them to *see* the answer, but in some instances the guides would actually have the subject feel the answer. That was the case with Shelly, who was working with a wolf and a spirit guide. As soon as I asked about the Divine, she immediately had an experiential response.

JS: We have terms like Divine, Source, Creator, God. What exactly is that?

Shelly: They're not telling me anything. They're making me feel it.

JS: Sometimes they do that. Sometimes they show people; sometimes they let you feel it. What do you feel?

Shelly: I can feel every cell in my body. I can feel the vibration and frequency in the energy just pulsing. It almost makes me nauseous and dizzy, it's so strong.

JS: When you say nauseous and dizzy, that doesn't sound like a good thing.

Shelly: I think it's because I don't think I've ever felt this much energy. It's just so strong. It's not scary. At first it was a little scary, but now I'm getting more acclimated to it.

Occasionally, when it was appropriate, I would give clients the opportunity to *feel* Divine energy during a session, and the response from Shelly was pretty typical. The feeling is very powerful and leaves a profound impression.

JS: What do you think the message is by having you feel this? Why do you think they're doing that? What are they telling you in answer to that question?

Shelly: To me it feels like the feeling that we are all one. I feel like they're spinning me.

JS: Are you okay?

Shelly: I am, but it's almost like being on a merry-go-round.

JS: Okay, let's have them take it down a little bit. What does this tell you about Source energy? Where is it?

Shelly: It's in the center of all of us.

JS: So we all have it?

Shelly: We all have it. I feel this spinning like to the point where it's trying to show me you can't separate us. As much as I would try to focus, all I can see is the blurs of how we are all so entangled and just this light.

JS: So there is a oneness about all of us?

Shelly: Yeah.

Shelly's experience wasn't unusual. Clients who have *felt* Divine energy often report that it is amazing, but a bit overwhelming. Shelly's guides may have chosen for her to undergo a sensory response because they felt it was the most convincing method they could use to answer the question. She was able to actually experience the energy firsthand and then sense that this energy is in all of us, without exception. As she observes, "You can't separate us."

Some people reading this might say that these are only a few examples, and they need more proof. Although only a handful of passages are presented in each chapter, it is important to remember that they are representative of the ideas that were expressed again and again in these sessions. I could have included hundreds of excerpts, but the sentiments expressed were so similar that the redundancy would have become tedious. When there were conflicting viewpoints on a topic, I included those, but one of the fascinating facets of these interviews was the incredible consistency of the answers.

With regards to this topic, *not a single session* generated an opposing viewpoint such as God and man are separate, or God is not forgiving and holds your sins against you, or there is only one path to God, or any other dogmatic beliefs expressed by some religions. Instead, this energy was all about connection, love, and forgiveness. And, many of the people who volunteered to participate in this process came from backgrounds which exposed them to very conservative religions. They could have echoed their early teachings, but that never happened.

Sometimes the language of the guides wasn't expressed in perfect, flowing English. The answer from Ryan's guides might not have been as eloquent, but it was consistent with what the other guides were saying.

JS: The first question I have is about the essence of God or Divine or Spirit or Creator, or whatever term you want to use. If that energy exists, what is the essence or nature of the Divine?

Ryan: You. You are the energy. You are the only thing. You are total love. You want to look further. You want to look up. You want to look elsewhere for it, but it is you. It is within. It is always within reach. It is the only thing within you. Real. Your true essence *is* God. It's you. It is what we fear because we don't understand.

JS: So, when you say that, are you saying that God's energy is in every one of us? Is that right?

Ryan: God's energy is in every one of us. All connected, all one, all bound by the spirit of love. No hate.

Time and time again, the Divine was described as "energy." Because this message described our connectedness and how Divine energy always regards us in "the spirit of love," it should be noted that Ryan's guide was Jesus.

Other commonly used words to describe Divine energy during these discussions were *love, oneness,* and *consciousness.* Consciousness, as described by Jerome, is a unifying energy. People often refer to the collective consciousness as thoughts or beliefs that run though all people.

JS: What about the essence of God or Divine or Spirit or Creator, or whatever term you want to use. If that energy exists, what is the essence or nature of God?

Jerome: Consciousness.

JS: What do you mean by that?

Jerome: Collective thoughts and awareness throughout the universe. All beings are connected. It doesn't matter about species.

JS: And what are they connected to?

Jerome: Just consciousness. Just being like a huge galaxy. Just light and all the colors.

JS: And we are all part of that? We're connected to that, is that what you're saying?

Jerome: We're all connected to that. And all worlds, all universes. We're all connected.

It might be interesting to note that Jerome came into his session describing himself as an atheist. The expectation, if the answers in these sessions were coming from our human minds, is that Jerome would have told us there is nothing out there and when we die we simply decompose. However, Jerome describes a connection we have on a grand scale, connected to "all worlds, all universes."

Given this notion of oneness and that all of us have Divine energy inside us, I had to ask about the validity of those who claim that only certain religions can lead one on the path to redemption. This strongly held tenet is still practiced by many faiths today. Nora's guardian angel typified the answers I received when I asked this question.

JS: Some people say that if you want to connect with God, you have to follow *our religion and only our religion*. What do you say about that: when they say the only path to God is through a specific religion?

Nora: It's silly.

There was a long pause, but I pressed Nora's angel for more information.

Nora: It's [Divine energy] there. You just have to let it in.

JS: There is no one path?

Nora: No.

When I began these interviews, I thought it was interesting how often the guides used the word *silly* when they responded to questions such as this one because that word, almost considered antiquated in contemporary language, came up a *lot* in these dialogues. As I thought about it more, I realized that was the perfect word to say "that is wrong" without coming from a place of judgment. After all, most people who have experienced that form of religious prejudice wouldn't use such a kind term to describe it and wouldn't be able to talk about that exclusionary practice without expressing some anger and frustration. And to follow that reply with, "It's there. You just have to let it in," is such a gentle way of suggesting we rethink some of these old convictions. One of the consistencies in these sessions was the way the guides always had a kind way of saying something wasn't right and doing so from a place of love and compassion.

Sylvia, a Christian client, was working with Jesus when I asked if there was only one path or one religion that leads to God.

JS: What about people from other cultures who are connected to Buddha or Allah or the Great Spirit in the sky? Are these all pathways that go in the same direction? Is it okay for people to have their own belief systems? Are they connecting with God in different ways?

Sylvia: So, Jesus is going to talk [Sylvia would announce who was giving the response before she relayed the information]: the most offensive verse in the Bible is "I am the way and the truth and the life." And that is 100 percent accurate, but people want to turn that into "you are in and you are out."

People want to use that against people, and that is not what that is intending. I will not let go of a single person.

It isn't uncommon for people to take passages from the Bible and use them, sometimes out of context, to further their own agendas. Some religions also engage in the practice of only accepting people who adhere to their specific belief system, but the most significant part of this passage is the last line: "I will not let go of a single person." That was a consistent theme throughout these sessions. Humans sometimes feel alienated or disconnected from the Divine, but the guides—whether it be Jesus Christ, the archangels, spirit guides, or even animal guides—always made it clear that they will never let go of anyone.

So, if we pull all of this information together, what conclusions can we draw about the nature or essence of the Divine? The answers from the guides differed greatly from what people had said in their pre-session interviews. Earlier in the book, I compiled opinions on this topic from people who were using their conscious minds and posted that information in a section called "The Participants." This is what was said when I asked people in the waking state about their spiritual beliefs:

## Information From Our Conscious/Waking Minds

| 30% | Are strongly connected to a religion (most often Christian-based). |
|---|---|
| 25% | Refer to themselves as "spiritual but not religious." |
| 20% | Are unsure about spiritually and don't know what to believe. |
| 13% | Don't believe in God or spirituality at all. |
| 12% | Feel a strong connection to the Earth energy, but aren't sure about God. |

Now if we compare those numbers to the information that came *from* the guides—and was stated by those very same individuals whose opinions made up the statistics above—it has a very different look:

## *Information From the Guides*

| | |
|---|---|
| 98% | The Divine is an energy in all of us and it is an energy that we all share with every living thing on this planet. It is all loving and forgiving. |

I'm saying 98 percent because there was a very small variance in the answers where guides got distracted or didn't clearly answer the question, but for all practical purposes, there was a universal agreement on this topic. Even the agnostics, the atheists, and those who were uncertain about the existence of God received information that was in alignment with that statement.

It should also be noted that there wasn't a single occurrence when the answer from a guide prefaced the response to this question with "I don't know," "That's a good question," or "I'm not really sure." Each time, the guides answered without hesitation or doubt.

Often, at the end of a session, I would use a process where clients could fully experience a heightened state of awareness and a deep direct connection with Divine energy. This is how one client described being part of that energy. Her account is an excellent representation of all the answers to this question. This is how she described the experience.

*I am a profound vessel of the Divine. I feel radiant. I feel heat. I feel so totally interconnected with everything. I feel the presence of this light. I feel the presence of all these beings, and there is no separation. This is it. This is the source of it all. We don't separate from this ever. We just forget.*

In conclusion, there were some very significant revelations that came to light because of this question. I'll start with what the guides said that is *not congruent* with many of our traditional beliefs.

- Under no circumstances was Divine energy ever said to be punishing or vengeful.

- The concepts of guilt, shame, and non-forgiveness were *never* supported by the guides and never a part of the dynamic we share with the Divine.

- Divine energy was never described in human terms or portrayed as a being, entity, or human form. There was never a gender associated with the Divine. It was unvaryingly described as an energy, never a person.

- There is no a single path, chosen method, or specific religion that should be followed in order to connect with Spirit. When I asked about religion, the guides were fine with whatever choice an individual might make as long as it was centered on love, peace, and compassion, and as long as it genuinely helped that individual align with Divine energy.

- It was clear that there is no separation between humans and the Divine. The idea that God is a separate entity looking down on us was not a part of the message of the guides. Instead, the message was that we are all one with the Divine.

Although that addresses many of the misconceptions about the Divine, what was in the communications that might help our understanding about the essence or nature of the Divine? What was the wisdom from the guides?

The most consistent message in response to these questions was that the Divine is "energy," and Divine essence is in every living thing. Divine energy is in all of us. There are no exceptions. There is no separation between the Divine and ordinary human beings. Not one guide varied from that message. And Divine energy, as I will discuss in future chapters, is also present in people who have done bad things.

A major part of our mission or purpose on this planet is to establish and maintain a solid—and genuine—relationship with that Divine energy. I use the word *genuine* because throughout history, people have misused the name of God and religion to support their own agendas. Genuine means that every day we are living our lives expressing the Divine energy within us. Every action we take should be taken with that connection in mind and Divine intention as our primary motivation.

Perhaps the most interesting observation about this process was the amazing consistency of the answers while in hypnosis. These replies did not in any way align with how people had answered this question with their conscious minds. There was no doubt or hesitation in the answers and never a hint of uncertainty about the existence of some form of Divine energy.

## Chapter 2

# What Happens When We Die?

Years ago, I traveled to another part of the country to attend the memorial services of someone who was very important in my life. Despite the fact that everything regarding the ceremonies went well, there was still a sense of coldness and isolation on that trip because we were in a place foreign to us and away from the comforts of our home. The hotel didn't feel particularly warm and cozy. The roads we traveled seemed lonely, the countryside felt more desolate than usual, and the weather was dreary and dark.

There were several components to the services. There was the viewing of the body, the memorial ceremony, and then the procession, a slow somber drive to the cemetery to say one last goodbye and actually see where the casket would eventually be placed into the ground.

Later that night, one of the family members solemnly said to me, "It makes me really sad to think about my father out there in the cold cemetery all by himself."

For a moment, I could relate to that chilling thought, as I imagined what it would be like to be out there in the cold and absolute darkness on your first night alone in a graveyard. I immediately felt a huge rush of sorrow—and even a moment of fear—as I thought about, and felt, that sentiment. What would it be like if that was me out there? Would there be a sense of overwhelming sadness? Would there be a feeling of complete loneliness as if you'd been abandoned? Would there be a claustrophobic experience during which you suddenly come to realize you are trapped inside a coffin and can't escape? Would there be ghosts or entities that haunted the cemetery?

And for many, whether they are picturing that scenario for themselves or for a loved one, those are the tremendously frightening and desolate images we associate with death. But is that really what happens when we die? Do we become a lonely spirit who roams the graveyard at night? Do we just go back into the earth and decompose? Is that last breath truly the end or is there something more?

Of all the questions for me to ask, this question was the one that could either provide the most comfort or broaden the fear that almost everyone on this planet has contemplated during their lifetime.

This is what the guides had to say when it came to what happens when we make our transition. Because there is so much anxiety around death, my first question for Whitney—and her goddess guide—and the initial question in the dialogues with several of the participants about death, addressed the fear around making a transition.

JS: Should we be afraid of death?

Whitney [laughing]: No.

JS: You laughed when I asked that. Why did you laugh?

Whitney: It's the limited thinking, the human experience. To us [the guides] is just…silly. There is no death.

As you read Whitney's last response, and noticed a missing word, it helps to remember that some of the responses of the guides aren't always expressed in perfect English.

JS: So what happens when we make our transition?

Whitney: The energy just shifts.

JS: Can you talk about that?

Whitney: It's just the physical body, the lower vibrations, falling away. Kind of like a butterfly, a caterpillar becoming a butterfly, just changing frequency.

It seems as if many of the misconceptions we have about life, death, and the afterlife are the result of our "limited thinking" as humans. In our culture, there is a great deal of fear, trepidation, and finality associated with passing away. To us, death seems to be a powerful ending point. It isn't uncommon for people to spend their entire lives with a subconscious fear of death. The guides look at it differently, like a caterpillar becoming a butterfly or perhaps a tree that goes dormant every winter only to come back and flourish the following spring.

In answering the question about mortality, the guides often referred to the physical experience of being human as a lower vibrational state and mentioned that it is difficult for the spirit to reside within the human body. They reminded us that the spirit form is our natural state and the human form is actually quite foreign to us. That was reinforced in the communication with Anthony's spirit guide.

JS: You talked [earlier] about making a transition. Should we be afraid of death?

Anthony: No, no, and no to all the fear of death and the darkness that accompanies fear.

JS: When we make our transition, what is that like? What is that experience like when you leave the physical body?

Anthony: It's like being set free. Your spirit is free of the density of a human body. It's in its light form, and its natural way of being. This [referring to the physical human form] is not natural. This is not a natural state of the soul. The soul is here using the body as a vehicle for whatever its purpose in the lifetime is.

When Anthony's guide says, "This is not natural," he is referring to our souls being enclosed within a physical body. A common message from these dialogues is that we are spiritual energies in a material world. One guide put this even more bluntly by summing it up this way: "You are not your body. You are energy."

John's guide alluded to this as well. When we leave the physical body we become more connected to the oneness in what John's guide refers to as our "normal state."

JS: A lot of people are afraid of dying and afraid of death. What happens when someone makes a transition? What do people need to know to help ease their minds?

John: In dying, fear is of the pain and of the unknown, not of death. Death is coming home. Death is moving away or releasing the limitations of who you truly are. You are lightness. You are being. You are love. The association of dying is with pain, not with release, not with abundance, not with a universal connectedness with all in terms of sending back to the normal state. You [humans] have done this as part of your control system. It is natural to fear the unknown when the separation is so intense and great, not so when the connectedness continues. It is the separation that you put in place for control. Not necessary. The higher you go in consciousness, your term [this was a reference to the word *consciousness* which I had used earlier in our dialogue], the better, the easier it is to understand the movement between ethers. Your restricted movement, your limited lesson life, your focus on the menial, makes this difficult to move in and out.

We think of death in terms of "separation." The guides are telling us that the "connectedness continues." We try to gain more "control" of what happens when we transition by trying to explain it, and understand it, in human terms. In reality, instead of trying to figure it out, it is probably better to trust that it is ultimately just another part of our journey. John's guide alludes to this notion when he says that there is an incredible sense of connection on the other side, and the reference to "movement between ethers" implies that there are other existences or incarnations that await us.

> JS: So If we focused on the connectedness and the love, there
>     would be no fear about the transition? It would be a
>     beautiful experience.
>
> John: It would be natural. It would be transcendental.

John's guide, who was Jesus, says that one of the problems people have with dying is that all of our focus is on the separation from the people and things that have become important to us in our lives. The implication of this answer is that if we actually knew and embraced how amazingly profound the connected feeling was when we make our transition, then it might actually be something to cherish. The association around death is always of loss. When someone passes, we are programmed to say to others, "I am sorry about your loss." Perhaps we should be looking forward to the love and connection we experience when we leave our physical bodies. That seems to be the implication from these communications.

Instead of being concerned with death and dying, the guides often talked about the journey of the spirit. Most of the guides seemed somewhat indifferent to the physical body. The human form wasn't important. Instead, the focus was always about the spirit, our learning, and our connectedness. Our essence or energy was always described as being united and connected. Never is the spirit floundering on its own—as we sometimes seem to do in human form. In every case, the spirit is rejoining the oneness or the whole. The Native American shaman working with Jason used a metaphor to describe the transformation process.

JS: What about people who are afraid of death? A lot of people here believe when you make your transition, you go into the ground and you're done. What does happen when we die?

Jason: If you're talking about a consciousness, no. We never die. If you're talking about an experience in an embodiment, yes we do. It is part of the evolvement experience in that you've chosen an embodiment, you are embodiment, and it's not a limited experience; however, there's only so far that you can experience within one embodiment, and at some point the being or consciousness sheds that so that they can take on another vehicle embodiment for whatever experience that being is choosing, for whatever experience that being is having experience.

We choose an embodiment—a human form—so that we can have a physical experience within which we can learn lessons that help us grow and evolve. There's only so much "you can experience within one embodiment," and then we need to "take on another vehicle embodiment" for the next set of lessons. More light is shed on this dynamic in Chapter 6, which addresses why we are here.

JS: So you can evolve to a certain degree, but that is as far as you can go within that body or that lifetime, and then you need to move on to evolve in a new manifestation or vehicle?

Jason: Yeah. You don't always want to stay in your parents' house. You could see that as an example of how that happens. The child is growing up in their parents' house, and in a "normal" experience, and at some point they've learned all the lessons that they're going to learn with their parents, and they need to leave the parents' house so they can experience the world for themselves. That process of leaving the house is that death experience in and of itself. It has nothing to do with that the consciousness of the child has died. Perhaps the awareness that they have at that moment has died as the experience expands for that child and their evolution. It has nothing to do with the love that the child has for those parents. Of course it's there.

Using the metaphor of the child leaving the parents' house might be a good way to look at the situation. In the moment when the child leaves the house, there is some sadness, but then the child or spirit evolves much like the butterfly emerging from the caterpillar as described in an earlier passage. That child has learned all he or she can within the confines of the parents' home and then moves forward.

Each of these responses was delivered as if the information was a commonly accepted principle. There was no sense of desperation, which would have implied there was finality or a true ending associated with transition. Instead, the replies to this question were often quite matter-of-fact, suggesting life and death are a cyclical part of our existence and not something to be feared.

When I questioned Carla's guide about death, her angel alluded to what was starting to become a common component within the answers to this question: each time a guide discussed this topic, there seemed to be some sort of reference to other existences. If that had only happened once or twice, it might have been overlooked, but almost every reply to this question furthered the notion that this life was only part of a larger continuum that is comprised of multiple existences. Carla's angel expanded on what was becoming a consistent stream of fascinating revelations about death and the afterlife.

JS: When we die, should we be afraid?

Carla: To die? No.

JS: Why not?

Carla: Because there's no end. There's no end. There is no fear of death because you're not going anywhere. It's not like you're stopping. You're not turning off the light. You're not ending the movie. You're just going into a different phase. It's all phases, and it's all cyclical. To die is to stop, but you're

not dying. You're just moving into a different phase, one that
you don't know yet because you haven't experienced it in
your consciousness. You have experienced it, in other lives,
but you haven't carried that recollection of it into this life to
give you that sense of comfort: "Oh, I'm just about to die. I
did this before." And if you had that, it would be really silly
at this point in your stage.

That statement—"You have experienced it [death], in other lives,
but you haven't carried that recollection of it into this life"—opened
up a whole new line of questioning. I had mentioned that this was
a journey of discovery—and surprises—for me. I did not expect the
answers about death to, in a very matter-of-fact tone, tell us "You've
died many times before, but you just don't remember." Carla's guide
tells us that we have no recollection of previous deaths, and if we
had a conscious memory of undergoing the transitional experience,
we would simply remember the process and accept it as a routine
event.

   The more I asked about death, the more commonplace it became
for the guides to start mentioning other planes of existence. Almost
every response in this chapter suggests that our present life is only
a small part of a much larger picture. I wanted to know more about
that, and much of that discussion comes in Chapter 3, but this final
excerpt, once again, mentions other planes of existence.

JS: What about those people who are afraid of dying? What do
   we tell them?

Janice: Dying is a change, and changes are frightening to many
   people, but it's just a change.

JS: Should we be afraid of it?

Janice: No. People focus on leaving other people and what
   the other people are going to do and how they're going to
   handle it, but it's just a change for them and once they do it
   they'll know, no biggie.

JS: You are implying that there is something more and the soul or spirit doesn't die.

Janice: No. [The "no" answer in this case is confirming the spirit itself doesn't die.]

JS: Just the physical body dies.

Janice: It's just the physical body.

JS: So the soul or spirit carries on?

Janice: Yes.

JS: Then, what happens next? Do we come back? Are there other existences?

Janice: There's a time of merging and a time of connectedness to other nonphysical beings. There's a time of reawakening to what our inner selves are really all about. Some go on to other planes and some come back [to Earth], but not all [come back to Earth].

Almost every answer to this question implied that there are other existences. Janice's guide mentions coming back to Earth or perhaps "other planes." It appeared that in order to reassure us humans that we should not be afraid of making our transition, the guides couldn't give us comfort or be convincing if they didn't allude to more existences beyond the here and now.

Despite the fact that only a handful of responses were included here, I could have easily included dozens more. Not a single respondent varied on this question. *Every* response assured us that there should be no fear around dying, and *every* answer went on to talk about how our true essence is spirit or energy. The human body and human experience were always described as just a temporary embodiment, whereas the spirit energy is forever.

One would have expected a wide variety of answers to this question because our conscious human minds have so many uncertainties around death. Earlier in the book, I described what would occur if we asked 50 people *in a conscious waking state* what happens to us when we die, and this was how I described it:

*Ten of those people might say you go to heaven. Ten might believe in reincarnation. Ten might suggest that you become part of a spiritual realm. Ten might say that you simply decay and go back into the earth. And, at least 10 would probably come back and say, "I don't know."*

But that wasn't what happened at all. There wasn't a single case in which a guide responded with "I don't know." In fact, there was complete uniformity in all of the answers. What this suggests is that we shouldn't be afraid of death. It isn't the ending. In many cases, death was described as a peaceful coming home or reconnecting to the oneness. One of the guides when describing the transition process reassured us, "...there will be many, many, many entities waiting to receive you and help you, and love you, and guide you to wherever your next existence will be."

## Chapter 3

# Do Parallel Planes Exist?

As I conducted the interviews for this book, there were many surprises. With some of the topics, my thought was: "I'll put that question out there, but I think I already know the answer." That was the case with parallel planes. I could accept concepts like reincarnation—coming back in another incarnation to learn more lessons—which to me was within the realm of possibility. However, the idea of parallel planes, where we could be in two places at the same time, always struck me as illogical. I had read about it and discussed it with people who believe in parallel planes, but I was never convinced. My mind works in a more linear fashion. It made sense to me that you would need to complete one lifetime before beginning the next.

Throughout the course of my life, the only indication I could find that parallel planes might exist were two types of phenomena that I had experienced. One was those unusual dreams we have that appear to be not of this world. I wondered if those could be glimpses or memory flashes from other existences.

I have also had times where just before waking from sleep, I would feel myself coming back into my earthly body. Sometimes that "settling in" phenomenon would be sudden and jarring. Other times, it would be gradual and take several minutes for me to reenter the physical form.

My assumption about this reentering my body upon waking was that—if indeed parallel planes were possible—my time away was allowing me to do work in another dimension. I was never exactly sure what that work or programming entailed. Perhaps it was a spiritual process where I was learning about my connection to Source. Maybe I was being taught new healing techniques to use in my practice. Maybe I was part of a group of healers working on healing the planet. But all of those thoughts were speculation, and that speculation didn't include being consciously in two places at the same time. It just opened up the possibility that I was going somewhere else, during my sleep, to work on some other level. There was no concrete evidence that when this phenomenon occurred I was really going anywhere, let alone that it had anything to do with simultaneous lifetimes or parallel planes.

So when I asked the guides about parallel planes, I fully suspected that the responses would support my personal perspective and confirm that we are not capable of existing in two places at the same time. After all, the only "evidence" I had was in the form of my own two examples that were no more than speculation.

I should clarify that, in respect to the questions for this chapter, I was really asking about two possibilities. First, I wanted to know if there were multiple dimensions. In other words, when we finish this lifetime, could we come back to Earth or perhaps start a new existence within some other plane or dimension. That line of questioning was based on the linear outlook in which, after you complete one lifetime, you could begin another.

The second question was the one that was illogical for me: could we experience parallel planes or simultaneous lifetimes?

One of the fascinating parts of this interview process was something I didn't expect: sometimes my clients would tell me that their guides would give them the answers long before I had finished asking the question. And there were other times when the guides would introduce a topic before I even brought up the subject. Such was the case with multiple and parallel planes. As I asked questions about what happens when we die, the conversation would quickly evolve to how this life was just one of many existences. The answers about death, as recorded in Chapter 2, would always begin by addressing how our spirits live on and only the physical body dies, but that was usually followed by a brief mention of how our spirits or souls move on to other incarnations. Because the issue of "other incarnations" was already on the table, I was curious to learn more, so I asked and they responded.

In the following conversation with Alex, who was getting information from Source, I hadn't asked about multiple or parallel planes. We were discussing death, but the actual question I had asked was if we should be concerned about a possible decline in the collective consciousness on our planet. In the answer, Alex's guide volunteered information I hadn't expected.

> Alex: Everything is working exactly as it's supposed to [with regards to the present state of affairs on Earth], and it's done this for trillions of years, not just on this planet, but on other planets, other galaxies, other universes. This has happened over and over and over. It's all part of a larger plan, a larger experience. It's simple, yet beyond our comprehension at the same time.

I quickly shifted my line of questioning from the concerns regarding the state of our planet to the subject of "other planets, other galaxies, other universes."

> JS: Are you saying that when we die, it's just the body that dies off, and the spirit exists on other planets, other universes,

other planes? We do all that? It's not just a short time on this planet and then we're done?

Alex: Source says there are no old souls. All souls are the same age. Some have more physical experiences than others. Some exist only in spirit. They never have a physical experience. Some only have physical experiences and rarely spend any time in the spirit realm, but each have their own agenda, their own experience they want to have.

Some clarification is necessary with regard to the statement: "Source says there are no old souls. All souls are the same age." The term *old souls* is one *coined by humans* in recent times to describe someone who we believe to be very evolved. That is a man-made descriptor. Apparently, based on this response, the age of a soul does not correlate to its level of evolution. As Alex's guide says, "all souls are the same age," which suggests that all of our souls or spirits have been around for a long time.

The more fascinating part of this exchange is the casual revelation about other planets, galaxies, and universes. There is a fair percentage of the population that embraces the idea of reincarnation in the context of coming back to this planet, but Alex's guide broadens the possibilities immensely to include other planes. Not only does that include other "universes," but it also includes spiritual realms where there is no physical manifestation.

In my conversation with Kathryn's guide, the topic of parallel planes, once again, came up unexpectedly. I had asked Kathryn's goddess-like spirit guide, what happens when people on Earth don't learn their lessons in this lifetime. Her guide was quick to point out that they can always learn those lessons or "awaken" at another time. I wanted the guide to be more specific about what was meant by "another time" because that response appeared to be a reference to multiple existences.

JS: When you say they're going to awaken at another time, does that mean that there are different lives, as in reincarnation, and if they don't get it this time, maybe they'll get it next time round?

Kathryn: Next life or some way...

JS: So there is more than one life?

Kathryn: Yes.

JS: And are those lives on this Earth or are they on different planes?

Kathryn: Yes. [Laughing.]

Kathryn's guides meant "yes" to both answers, and it was as if she were laughing at my surprise.

JS: Can you explain?

Kathryn: Different planets. Different planes. Different dimensions. It's all going on, all the time.

JS: Are there what we call parallel planes? Are we living in more than one place at the same time?

Kathryn: Yes.

JS: How can that be?

Kathryn: The Universe is happening all at the same time. You are truly a multidimensional being with limited understanding. It doesn't translate. It's something you have to allow yourself to feel.

JS: So we could be here in this moment doing this, but we could also be working on some other plane at the same time?

Kathryn: Yes. You are.

JS: And fully conscious and aware there just as we are here?

Kathryn: Yes.

JS: And what about time? Could we [referring to Kathryn and myself] both be artists from the Renaissance at the same time that we're here?

I picked "artists from the Renaissance" randomly, but my objective was to see if we might be simultaneously experiencing these different periods of time.

> Kathryn: Yes, time is just another thing that man created to control.

I wanted more clarification.

> JS: Concurrently, we could be experiencing different times and different planes?
>
> Kathryn: Yes.
>
> JS: So, we don't necessarily have to "get it" on this plane because we might be figuring things out somewhere else?
>
> Kathryn: Yes.
>
> JS: Can you tell me a little more about how this all works?
>
> Kathryn: The soul is fragmented into spirits, into spirit. Each lifetime that's going on is a piece of the soul; it's that particular spirit or energy. So you have your oversoul or higher self, directing all of this at once.

Kathryn's guide's use of the word *oversoul*, in this case, is being used to describe the part of our spirit that governs or oversees our individualized spiritual journeys. Not only were multiple planes of existence mentioned in the answer, but the notion of simultaneous or parallel planes were mentioned almost as if it were common knowledge.

These ideas certainly challenge our commonly accepted societal perceptions, but should our beliefs always be fashioned after what is socially appropriate or scientifically provable, especially when we are dealing in a realm where almost nothing is provable? Our primary source of information when dealing in this realm has always been religious doctrines that reflect beliefs that are centuries old and, in many cases, fashioned to discourage freedom of thought. At an early age we are taught to imagine that there is God, heaven, a devil, and hell, but then, under no circumstances, are we to imagine anything beyond that. But what if we did? What if we were a society of free thinkers who were open to all possibilities? Would the notion of other dimensions and simultaneous existences be so unfathomable?

In Chapter 2, most of the answers that addressed what happens when we die described how the physical body dies off, but the spirit or energy inside us moves on to other dimensions. Most people probably assumed that meant reincarnation on Earth or perhaps a merging of the soul with the energy of the Divine. But as I asked more questions, not only do other planets, planes, and universes get introduced, but also the possibility that we might be multidimensional beings experiencing these various planes all at the same time. Ann's spirit guide described how our learning or evolution occurs in multidimensional layers.

JS: Are we doing it [learning and evolving] just on this planet, or are there other existences or planes or planets?

Ann: Many, many, many dimensions, many planets, many universes. It is unending.

JS: We don't even have a clue about how large this is?

Ann: No, and not supposed to in the human form.

JS: Why not?

Ann: Because the brain and the density of the human being is not able to handle the vibrational frequency of a higher being.

JS: So this is a lower state for us?

Ann: Yes.

Even though I was a bit surprised by the answers I was getting, most of the guides acted as if this was common knowledge. There was no indication that they were giving up closely guarded secrets; they were very forthcoming on this topic. The bigger problem was their frustration in trying to explain the concept in understandable language that humans can comprehend and accept. As Ann's guide says, because the human brain is not able to handle the higher vibrational frequency, we are not able to easily understand our multidimensional nature.

Other guides mentioned our inability as humans to comprehend our multidimensional nature. Perhaps this is why we have little or no conscious memory of our previous existences or our connection to the Divine when we come onto this planet. Alexandra's guide, an angel immersed in blue light, spoke of how our human physical state is too consuming for us to embrace or remember our other existences.

JS: Are there other dimensions, other planes, other existences, or is it just our short time on this Earth?

Alexandra: There are other planes and dimensions; however, when we choose this physical life on this plane, it's like we give up our ability to connect with those. When we choose to be in this physical body in this dimension, it's a big assignment and there's much to be focused on and it becomes difficult to understand or—it's hard to describe this—there are many dimensions and we are connected through universal love and it's like a web of energy that connects us, but in our restrictive physical state in this life it's more difficult for us to communicate with those other aspects.

JS: Those other existences or dimensions, are we experiencing those simultaneously with our existence here?

Alexandra: Yes, everything is in every moment.

JS: So our light or energy, might be in several places—different planes, different existences—at one time?

Alexandra: Yes, but that's different manifestations of the energy field, so we would often not understand or relate to those other expressions.

JS: Is it possible that Alexandra is here now in 2016, but at the same time is also a painter in the Renaissance or someone who lived in England in the late 1700s? Are we on multiple planes like that at the same time?

Alexandra: Yes. There is no time.

Alexandra's guide says that being in the physical form in this human dimension makes it very difficult to understand and grasp our existence in other dimensions. The guide also ends with a statement that had started to emerge more and more in these dialogues: "There is no time." I began to realize that, to fully understand the concept of multiple planes, I was going to have to delve into a completely different perspective about the construct of time, a construct that may not be congruent with what we've grown to accept. That discussion happens in Chapter 9, but first I needed more information about multiple dimensions.

Janice's guide was Jesus. One of the concerns I mentioned earlier was if the guides associated with a specific religion would only respond in a way that was compatible with that faith. For example, would Jesus, acting as a guide for a client, only embrace Christian ideology? This question created a perfect opportunity to find out the answer to that concern.

JS: Are there other worlds out there, other planes?

Janice: Yes, most definitely.

JS: Is there any way you can describe that in human language: what is it like on those other planes?

Janice: There are many and they are varied. Some are very enlightened and able to see and understand and hear the universe and what's happening in the universe. Other planes are in some ways similar to the Earth's existence, but lighter, more enriching to what you call the soul.

JS: So it's not like we just plunk down on another planet and have a similar experience to Earth; these are more spiritual realms?

Janice: We are lighter beings. The Earth's existence is a heavier existence, almost cumbersome. There are other planes where it's not quite so heavy.

From this answer, it appears that a guide like Jesus *can* respond without being limited to a specific set of doctrines. Although these ideas may not be consistent with some of today's Christian beliefs, we don't know conclusively that these ideas weren't a part of the original Christian doctrines; after all, the Bible throughout history has undergone several rewrites, transformations, and omissions of its original text.

Why would the guides be so forthcoming about this topic? It almost felt like this intelligence was being freely shared for a purpose. In the past, multiple lives and parallel planes always seemed to be one of those mysterious subjects that "normal people" never talked about, yet there was absolutely no restraint when it was addressed in these sessions. As I got more into the interview process, an answer, or should I call it speculation, came to my mind. It almost felt that *if* the guides could convince us that there are many existences beyond our present one and let us know that this is not the end, *then* our collective attention might shift from a concentrated focus on this lifetime, and death in this lifetime, to the bigger picture of our evolution on a grander scale. In other words, if we knew this was one of many lives and our true objective throughout millennia was to become beings of love and light, would we be so focused on the here and now? Would we be obsessed about what we can get out of this one lifetime or would we open up our consciousness to become more mindful of a deeper connection with Divine energy? Have the traditional beliefs about life and death actually held us back from progressing spiritually? Would our entire perspective change if the awareness of our multidimensional nature replaced the belief that we have one life and one existence? I wondered if the open disclosure of these vast dimensions was deliberate. Had we tapped into something that on the surface seemed like a guarded secret, but in reality was information they actually wanted us to have in order to redirect the focus of our existence from the self to the collective energy?

That seemed to be the implication of this discussion with Neil's guides. The intent of this passage appears to be changing our focus from our present existence to the bigger picture. In this case, the emphasis was on learning lessons in order to become more enlightened.

JS: Can you talk about existences in other realms?

Neil: Everything is love and light. Light moves quickly. Everything can move quickly as we are light within and love with all. There are many lessons to learn. Not all can be learned here. This realm, this consciousness, these limitations, as you begin to understand the vastness, the connectedness, the structure of all you understand, the elements can change depending on the determinations needed for you to keep advancing, keep your energy expanding. For this, you need different energetic realities. Those are found everywhere. This is one. This is limiting. Light is a huge one that you miss here. It is the one that you must go elsewhere to master.

Apparently, we need these different planes or "energetic realities" to learn our lessons and to fully evolve. We have grown accustomed to thinking of everything within the limited context of our lives on Earth because it is all we can scientifically *know or measure,* and our society has for the most part taken a scientific approach to the way we look at the universe. But science had also convinced us that we *aren't* made up of energy, the mind and emotions have nothing to do with our physical health, and that the Earth was square. Perhaps our limited thinking has convinced us that other planes don't exist because no concrete evidence has ever been produced. The problem with that scientifically based thinking is that growth in the spiritual realm is reliant on immeasurables such as love, trust, energetic connections, and faith.

In compiling this work, I decided to be open-minded in my approach. Instead of denying what can't be scientifically proven, I was open to new information and new ways of looking at this subject; after all, the concept of these other realities hadn't just come up in one or two sessions: the existence of multiple dimensions had started to become a regular part of every dialogue with every guide. So, I wanted to know more. I wanted to know *how* it would be possible for us to consciously exist in more than one place at a time. This was the concept of parallel planes. How could that be possible, I wondered?

One of the guides explained the process of parallel planes by comparing our spirits to giant microorganisms. He said our soul was like a giant amoeba with lots and lots of tentacles. Each tip of each tentacle could be experiencing a different life, but each of those lives is still connected to the central body of the amoeba, which represents the spirit or the soul.

I asked Chris, communicating with Source, about parallel planes and how it could be possible for our souls to be in more than one place at the same time.

JS: So, we are experiencing different dimensions all at the same time?

Chris: Yes.

JS: One soul part of Chris is here now, but there might be another part of him that is experiencing a whole different lifetime, is that correct?

Chris: Yes.

JS: People refer to things like parallel planes. Is it possible that Chris could be having simultaneous existences on this planet? Could he be a farmer in the Philippines or a teacher in India while he is in this chair at this particular time?

Again, I picked these scenarios at random, but this time I was asking if Chris could be in multiple places on Earth *concurrently* with *this* lifetime.

Chris: Yes, absolutely.

JS: It feels like we have consciousness here, but the soul must have multiple states of consciousness or be able to be conscious or present in many places at the same time because you are fully aware in these different places. Is that right?

The guides answered this by pointing out that there is a paradox in our understanding of oneness or connection. Although we are all connected, there are aspects to each of us that can be quite unique.

Chris: Yes and here is part of the paradox: On the one hand, all sentient beings, people on this planet, we are all connected, so there is that layer of connection. On the other hand, there are different expressions of who we each are and who we're connected with.

JS: You're saying there are lots of other dimensions as well?

Chris: Absolutely.

I started to wonder, if our soul could concurrently be inside more than one person on this planet, would it be possible for two people who embody the same soul to come in contact with one another. Perhaps they would be drawn to each other or feel a deep connection. I had to ask:

JS: Could a husband and wife be the same person or share the same soul?

Chris: Yes.

This opens up the concept of soul mates. That term most likely has its roots in Plato's *Symposium*, in which humans were essentially split in two parts and each of those parts is looking for its mate or other half. Unfortunately, through the years, the term has lost its significance because of the overuse it has received in the last few decades. In the recent past, anytime two people began a new relationship and went through the honeymoon phase, they would quickly declare that they had found their soul mate. More often than not, after a year or so when the glow had worn off and the relationship was over, that same "soul mate" had been recategorized as a loser.

But the implication behind this type of soul mate is a little different. What if two people who were at the ends of two different tentacles connected to the same amoebic soul had somehow found each other, either by accident or design? Many of us have experienced a relationship in our life where we felt so close to the other person, it seemed uncanny. An example might be the husband and wife who, after many decades, were still as madly in love as the way they were the day they met. It could be a young boy who felt extremely connected to his grandfather or maybe even two lifelong, inseparable friends.

Rather than using the amoeba example, another guide explained how it was possible for us to be operating on parallel planes using a different illustration, and the best English word the guide could find was *fractionation*, which means to break up or divide up into smaller portions. So, perhaps our soul, while still maintaining its original essence, can separate into smaller pieces and those pieces can be simultaneously present in different embodiments.

I mentioned that not all guides agreed that our souls can be experiencing two planes of existence simultaneously. This guide's perspective is an example of how there was a very small level—less than 5 percent—of dissent, because the guide working with Stephanie indicated that parallel planes might only be possible for souls with higher levels of enlightenment and connection. It is interesting to notice that my question was actually about spiritual support, and it was the guide who volunteered the information about parallel planes.

JS: What's helping us on the other side? In other words, what can we tell them [readers of this book] in regards to angels or spirit guides? What is on the other side? Who's helping us?

Stephanie: It is different for some souls, but we all have spirit guides. What is known as God, the Divine, is always there for all. Some that have parallel incarnations, this will be very difficult to understand, but those who are advanced enough to have parallel incarnations, those parallel incarnations can actually talk back and forth and help each other. It's one soul, but it's like the soul has different personalities across different dimensions. Then they have a different level of guidance, for they also have their spirit guides, but then they have the different segments of expression that are helping them. And, of course, the Divine is always there for all of us.

JS: Interesting. So it's like you could consult with yourself if you're on a different plane?

Stephanie: Many people do when they are sleeping at night. The astral projection that many talk about where they leave their body, they are actually astral projecting and sensing or trying to join with another aspect of expression on another plane. It's very difficult to explain.

JS: Is that pretty common, in our sleep, that we're doing work?

Stephanie: For some souls, it is very common.

Perhaps this is that feeling I described of coming back into your body just moments before you wake up.

JS: When you say some souls are in parallel existences, how much of the population does this? What percentage of the population? Are most of us doing this?

Stephanie: It shifts. It shifts according to the awareness of the soul. An awareness, a consciousness can expand or contract. It can expand unlimitedly once it leaves the physical body. In the physical body it can only expand so far and then it can no longer be in a physical body, but there can also be some contraction sometimes when the soul loses its way because of the overwhelming experience of something that's happened in the physical body to the soul. The vocabulary is very limiting to be able to really put forth these ideas in an understandable context.

Stephanie's guide implies that more dimensions are available to those who are more evolved. It sounds like those advanced souls may actually be able to communicate with themselves from one realm to another. It is also interesting that, as I discussed in the introduction to this chapter, we may be communicating with other dimensions during our sleep.

One of the most remarkable experiences I witnessed during these interviews happened early on in this process during a discussion of parallel planes. It involved Danielle, who was working with her master guide.

JS: Are there multiple lives?

Danielle: Um-hm.

JS: And we have lessons to learn?

Danielle: Lessons. As we learn, we change, we shift. He [her guide] says it's not always human life. As we learn, the lesson, we move up and on.

Danielle was referring to her master guide when she said "he," and the way this master guide responded to questions was to show Danielle various scenes. In other words, rather than telling her the answer, he would often take Danielle to a scene to allow her to see or experience the answer for herself.

JS: When you say, not always human life, this implies that we may come back to Earth or we may go somewhere else?

Danielle: We can come back as an animal. He's showing me (I'm trying to wait for him to stop). We can come back as a guide. Once we've learned our lessons here, we can come back as different energy in a different planet, different solar system. He says, look at me: I am not from the Earth, but I am your master. He said I was a star child, which I did find out just recently, and he says that's my example.

JS: Are some of these lives going on simultaneously as in parallel planes? Can we work on multiple levels, or are we here just to do one thing at a time?

There was a moment of silence, then a long exhale. Danielle's face lit up and it almost felt that there was a radiance coming from her being. I could tell something had changed.

Danielle [after a long exhale and an expression of brightness and lightness]: He took me to a different plane. [Whispering.] It's very high. It's very light.

JS: Can you tell me about that?

Danielle [whispers]: It's very hard to talk. The frequency is very high. The vibration is taking time for me to get used to. So he shows me, that's the answer to your question. He took me to where he says I work at night. Although I am here on Earth physically, I can be in different planes at the same time.

JS: What was that like for you?

Danielle: I'm still there.

JS: How is it?

Danielle: I wanna stay here. It's just so high.

JS: When you say high…

Danielle: The vibration is just sooooo different. All I can see is I feel like I'm in the universe and its night and everything is sparkling and shining, and I'm sparkling, like I'm a star. [With surprise.] Oh my gosh, I'm a star! He sends me to show me my stuff. Wow. [Laughing.] He said he knows I enjoy it here, but we should go back.

That opened the door as far as I was concerned. From that point on, as long as it was safe and everyone involved had granted permission, I was going to develop a process that would enable my clients to visit another plane. Not all the guides or subjects were willing, but most were, and the response from many of the clients after the session was that the experience was life-changing. Here is the way Jessica described her trip to another realm.

JS: Are you able to experience another plane; is that possible? Just a glimpse to see what it's like.

Jessica: So far, all I see are lots of little lights and rainbow lights.

JS: That's similar to what others said. What does it feel like?

Jessica: It definitely has more energy and busyness feeling than what the in between place did.

When Jessica refers to the "in-between place," she was comparing it to what it was like when she visited the state that exists between lives.

Jessica: It's very busy in a much lighter way. Lots of energy and beings.

JS: What kind of beings?

Jessica: They mostly don't have form. They're just energies, beings of colors, and are doing things. Some are helping people on Earth. Some are doing things in the ether or the plane where we are. It's very light. Much lighter.

JS: What's your takeaway from this plane? If you were residing there, what would be your objective or mission or what would you be trying to accomplish?

Jessica: I wouldn't have to do anything. I could rest if I wanted. I could do things. First they would want to reorient me back to there before I did anything.

JS: Do you feel emotions as strongly? I've had people who said if you really want to feel love, you need to come to this planet.

Jessica: To the Earth planet?

JS: Yes. Or does this plane also feel very loving?

Jessica: Love is not the right word. It's full of light and peace, but not the peace we think of. Very full of light, lightness, which is love and peace and everything all at once.

JS: That sounds fabulous.

Jessica: It is fabulous. They just say it's not easy for people to come there, though, because it's hard to be in it if we've been too attracted to all the intensity down here.

I never expected to get information about parallel planes, let alone have my clients actually experience those other dimensions. Although the visits were brief, it felt like the guides really wanted us to know and embrace these other realities. Again, perhaps that was an attempt to get us away from our preoccupation with our material world.

Alberto went to another plane without any prompting from me. It was a spontaneous regression. It seemed like the guides wanted to take the clients there, and perhaps part of this movement was that something about experiencing that other dimension was important for the client's personal journey. This was Alberto's account.

Alberto: I see a ringed planet, and I feel the warmth from it.

JS: Guide, is it okay for Alberto to see and experience this?

Alberto: Yes.

JS: Guide, can you guide him and tell Alberto why he's here and what he's supposed to experience?

Alberto: This is a sample, sample of other realities.

JS: So you can see what it's like on another realm?

Alberto: Another realm, another world.

JS: Alberto, let yourself feel that for a second and tell me what it's like.

Alberto: It's beautiful. I can feel myself floating and looking up and seeing this ringed planet that has all these bands of blue and green, and I feel in love with life. And I'm high up in the air.

JS: Is that okay?

Alberto: Oh yeah! It feels wonderful to feel the wind beneath my wings.

JS: And why does your guide want you to feel this?

Alberto: He wants me to know that there is life beyond this, that there is happiness, that there's awareness beyond this life. I might not recognize it when I see it, and it may be part of me now.

JS: Is it possible that Alberto is on this other plane and working on the Earth at the same time?

Alberto: Yes.

JS: Guide, what do you say about that?

Alberto: Yes, it's very possible. There are so many different planes of reality and we exist on multiple dimensions.

I reminded Alberto, at the end of the session, that although he was open-minded, he described himself as an atheist and didn't necessarily believe in such things as guides, souls, or other incarnations.

If you took a survey and asked people on the street about the existence of parallel planes, you would probably first have to explain the concept, and even then, it is doubtful that too many would buy into the notion. There was a very small percentage, less than 5 percent, of the guides that didn't fully support the concept of parallel planes—where we could be in two places at the same time—but almost 100 percent of the guides talked openly about other dimensions. There was no mystery in these communications: other planes of existence were commonly accepted and discussed. One of the guides summed it all up this way:

*This is not all there is. This is only all we can
sense at the moment.*

*There are much greater levels of existence.*

It never felt that this information was given to surprise or shock us. It was always framed in a way where we were reminded that this is how we learn and evolve. Some guides expressed this as becoming love and light; others talked about how we become a more integral part of a greater consciousness. There was often a difficulty in expressing the concept in human terms, but it was always conveyed in a way to reassure us that there is a loving and caring energy out there and, by nature, that is what we are to embody and express in our own individual essences and in our everyday lives.

It is difficult to wrap the human mind around these concepts. How could there be many planes? How could there be simultaneous existences? I didn't understand it or accept it until a stream of people came through my office and, under hypnosis, their guides explained it to me. If it had been one or two, I might have been skeptical, but when the same information came forth in dozens and dozens of sessions, I had to start paying attention. And this information wasn't just from the guides of the metaphysical clients; it came from people who strongly disagree with such things. It didn't just come from spirit guides; it came from *all* guides, including the ones associated with specific religions.

So why are we resistant to consider such things? Many of our beliefs about other realms have been stifled by the scientific community who say that if you can't prove it, it doesn't exist. However, we can't prove there is a Divine energy and yet most people believe in that. And, we are dealing with a realm where almost nothing is provable.

Perhaps the other more powerful force that keeps us from considering such things is organized religion. For most of us, the most influential exposure to beliefs about God and the afterlife came early in our lives and were imparted to us by organized religions. They told us what we were, and more importantly, what we were *not* supposed to think. We weren't encouraged to think for our-selves. We were told our beliefs must fall in line with the teachings of the church.

So, with this information from the guides, we have the opportu-nity to come up with our own ideas and conclusions. If we go back in history, there have been times when society told us things we were supposed to embrace such as the concept of segregation. What if we didn't have those free thinkers who resisted those beliefs?

If we accepted the idea that we are multidimensional beings hav-ing simultaneous existences, it would change the way our society has traditionally viewed death and the afterlife. I asked Bridget's guide if we should rethink this perception.

JS: Here [in our earthly existence], we see death in terms of finality; you die and it's all over. It sounds like what you're saying is that concept is misguided.

Bridget: Because of the density [of the human form or body] and what that doesn't allow you to see, and the religions and the things that say to you "there is one time," and they've convinced people that they can't see how many iterations or entities occur at one time, so they [people] don't understand there is nothing to fear [about death] if there are so many places that any one energy can exist all at the same time.

The guide begins by affirming that the density of the human form makes it nearly impossible to remember or comprehend our multi-dimensional nature. This confirms the statements made by other guides which had come up earlier in this chapter. Then, there is the comment about religions and the ongoing encoding, which says, "there is one time," a reference to the assertion that we live and die only once. Finally, there is the phrase that says, "They've convinced people that they can't see how many iterations or entities occur at one time," which is probably a reference to societal and religious programming that has limited our ability to think freely about the possibility of multiple existences.

The inference in this guide's reply is that if we have an infinite number of existences and if the spirit or soul is immortal, then death truly is "nothing to fear." When I tried to pull all of this information together and get the guide to confirm that we shouldn't be afraid of death, Bridget's guide responded with this analogy: "That's [being afraid of death is] like being upset that a single cell in your body sloughs away."

# Chapter 4

# Do We Stay Connected to Those Who Are Close to Us?

One of the commonly used tools in hypnosis is a process called age regression, in which the client goes back to an earlier time in their *current* life in order to process a traumatic event or harmful imprint that might in some way be blocking that individual from reaching their full potential. It is often used to release negative beliefs related to that incident or to help that person understand why the event occurred and what they were supposed to learn in order to move forward on their journey.

I have done age regression thousands of times in my practice, so when I attended a seminar and had a chance to actually participate in the process, where I was the one undergoing the experience and not the facilitator, I was really looking forward to it.

When the session began, I went back to a time when I was probably about 6 years old, and our extended family had gathered for a picnic in the local park. It had been a warm, still summer day, and this park, spread out over rolling green hills, had tall mature trees accented by beds of colorful flowers. I remembered rolling down those grassy hills with the other kids, giggling, getting dizzy, and running back to the top so I could do it again. There were other scenes that came up as well: visions of the family together, eating dinner, talking, and sharing.

Initially, I wasn't sure about the significance of this memory. As a practitioner who facilitates age regressions, I expected to return to a traumatic event or some sort of crisis that would require emotional healing, but, for some reason, I had gone back to what, by all appearances, was a good time. I was with other cousins and family members whom I liked, and I felt connected.

It wasn't customary for our extended family to gather like this. In looking back, it must have been an important birthday or anniversary. As for me, I was back at a time where I was just being a kid. Most of my focus was on running around and playing, but there was also a part of me that enjoyed the fact that I was gathering with this tribe of people. It felt like *my* tribe, and it felt like these people would forever be an ongoing part of my life.

Our family had been fractured into different factions by divorce, so these gatherings were often small and usually would include only one branch of the family tree. This time it included the elders from my father's side of the family, a group that had a profound impression on my life.

My great aunt was there. I saw her as the matriarch of the family, but she assumed that role in a quiet, gentle way. She didn't rule with an iron fist; she led with her heart. It was from her that I learned about unconditional love, something she lived and practiced every day. You could feel it in her presence.

There were other elders, who probably would be classified by genealogists as cousins. One of those cousins was always full of joy. She had a calmness about her and a beautiful laugh, and she always had a way of making you feel at peace. From her, I was to learn about the importance of having a sense of lightness in one's being, something I feel like I am still fully trying to grasp.

Yet another elder was a more mysterious cousin. She was the intuitive one. She knew things that she shouldn't have known. She was probably very psychic, but in those days, such things were never discussed or practiced openly. From her, I learned it was okay to explore and nurture the mystical and spiritual side of myself.

To clarify, never was a word spoken by these elders as a means to teach me any of these lessons. These qualities were a part of their being, and the teaching was all intuitive. I observed how they lived and on some level knew what was to be taken in by my spirit or soul. At the time, I wasn't tangibly aware of any of their gifts or influence. I knew that there was something I admired in those people, but I only came to understand the power of their influence as I have looked back at my life years later.

So, there I was, returning to a setting where life—at that moment—felt pretty good. My practitioner mind kept trying to step in and decipher what all this was all about. I was looking for something to process or heal, but by all appearances, I had simply returned to a peaceful summer evening when I was spending time with people who were important to me.

I continued to search for answers. I know from facilitating this process with clients that the subconscious always goes to scenes that are significant. There is always a reason or lesson. Nothing about this process is random.

And then I got some awareness about the situation. I felt some sadness about this experience as I realized it might have been the last time we were ever all together in one place as one united family. There were divorces, relocations, illnesses, and eventually deaths that rapidly scattered everyone in different directions. There was strength when the group was together—which might have been why it felt so right—but we were never together again after that night. I saw most of those people one-on-one again, but this last gathering was the end. We were never together again as a tribe.

When I think of those elders today—now that they have all passed on—it is with some sorrow, but also great fondness. I think about what I could have learned from them had we spent more time together, but also I feel gratitude for what I did gain from being around them in the short time we did share. They never sat me down and taught me specific lessons. I learned from who they were. In a sense, they were like living, breathing guides for me, existing on the same plane as I was; it wasn't like we were trying to connect as guides and humans from different dimensions.

People who have had near-death experiences report that when they cross the veil, they are met by someone who they felt close to in this life. I've often wondered—when I make my transition—if those elders will be the people to greet me on the other side. And would I—in some other dimension—ever see them or be with them again?

So, the next question I pondered while doing this work was if I would ever see those elders again, or for that matter, would I see my more immediate family again beyond this short-lived earthly encounter. Do we briefly cross paths with the people we know and love for one short lifetime, or is there a stronger connection in which we meet again in other incarnations? Based on the information revealed by the guides in the first couple of chapters, we have been told we have multiple existences, but do we interact with the people we were close to in this lifetime on one of those future planes? Will I ever share time again with those elders? What about other close relationships I've had in this life? I had to know the answer to that question, so that became the next topic for discussion: do we stay connected to those who are close to us?

Kyle was working with Source during his session when I asked him about the connections we have to other people we meet in this lifetime. Kyle had been talking about how we exist on multiple planes—something consistent with the communications in the previous chapters—when I asked his guidance if we maintain our relationships throughout those multiple existences.

JS: Do we go through these different existences with the same group of people? Kyle and his wife are very connected in this life. Do they go through several planes together, or is it just a onetime meeting and then you move on?

Kyle: We're like geese. We fly together. We're like a flock. Sometimes we don't interact with the same people in each incarnation. We might miss them for a couple of incarnations and then they'll be back later on. Some we deal with almost every time, both in negative and positive ways. You would be surprised how many people you meet in the course of your life that you had known in other lives, if only briefly. It might've been your barber a hundred years ago and that's all you interacted with them, but you still meet them today, and you know each other on the soul level. Every time you meet somebody that you immediately like or you immediately dislike, there's a reason for that. Very few people come into our life as neutrals, but remember that each person's oversoul [the oversoul is often described by guides as sort of a director of a soul's journey] knows each other's oversoul, so you have that familiarity in that regard too.

Kyle's analogy of a flock of geese is very appropriate. We might be with our flock for a time, get separated for a while, rejoin the flock, form a subgroup that goes in a different direction, return to the flock, and so on. In a sense, each of these deviations is like a different lifetime, but we keep reconnecting with our same group of souls, which is referred to as our soul group or soul family.

Kyle's guide also mentioned that we meet people we immediately like or dislike. It is important to understand that our soul family includes people with whom we can have loving connections as well as individuals who can be minor antagonists in our lives. Most of our lessons are going to come from encounters with our adversaries. If you watch a flock of geese, there are some birds that are comfortable together and other geese that often pick on each other.

The connection or *knowing* of other individuals is often described as more of an energetic knowing because our bodies and personalities from this incarnation don't carry over into other dimensions. Once we cross the veil, we shed the character we played in this earthly drama. We are like a group of actors that assume different roles in each existence. So, we recognize the energy of someone we've known in the past, but we don't necessarily associate a personality with that being because that character changes with each manifestation. Cameron's guide, an angelic female, describes our energetic knowing in a passage that starts with my response to her guide's assertion that death is not the end and should not be such a big deal for us.

JS: She [Cameron's guide] says that death isn't a big deal, but what about the people that we're close to such as family members or friends? Do we see them again?

Cameron: We know their energy. We know their source, their essence, so they're familiar to us. We don't necessarily see them in their bodies.

JS: Do we stay with the same groups? Could we experience another lifetime with them? Do we stay together with the same spirits or souls?

Cameron: Um-hm. Um-hm. We know them. We feel affinities for them, and we also meet other energies as well. But we connect, we do have senses and experiences with like energies, they are familiar.

The guide refers to this as "energies" we are familiar with, not people we have known. This is probably a more accurate description. For example, the *energy* who played the part of a sister in one life might return in a subsequent life as an inseparable friend. And the two beings who have that amazing connection on one plane will often maintain that bond even though variables, such as personality traits, might differ dramatically from one existence to the next.

On the opposite side of the spectrum, this might also explain people in relationships that, on the surface, appear to be grossly mismatched. We have all witnessed or personally experienced relationships that are enabling or abusive or appear to be completely unfulfilling. Perhaps this is the result of a connection or contract between two souls that have been interacting for many lifetimes and what seems on the surface to be a dysfunctional connection is all part of the evolution of those two souls. They have agreed to play out their incompatible relationship to learn from one another. Outsiders, who know them, may become frustrated as they can look at the situation objectively, whereas the two players involved may take an extended period of time to fully embrace the lesson that comes from that dysfunctional relationship; thus, they participate in the discord far longer than they should. Additionally, there are those who, in this lifetime, will never find resolution in the situation because they have decided to ignore their lessons. To our human minds, it will appear that they never "get it" and stay mismatched throughout their entire lives. There is much more about lessons in Chapter 5.

Cameron's guide also mentioned that "we also meet other energies." Sometimes others—those who are not a part of our soul family—can come into our soul group from time to time to play specific roles. These transient energies might have an assignment that cannot be fulfilled by one of the soul family members. When the outsiders' work is done, they can return to their own group. A positive example of this might be a highly evolved soul that comes in to act as a teacher to one of the group members who is studying spirituality. Perhaps that group member is going to make a gigantic evolutionary leap in this lifetime, but the teaching needs to come from a being who is more evolved than any of the present members of that soul family.

There can also be negative beings, who are not from our soul families, but are needed to participate in a lifetime to help someone learn their lesson. The earlier passages indicated that we will have minor antagonists that come from our soul families, but sometimes a lesson might call for a major antagonist, such as an abusive or malevolent individual, and that person will often need to come from outside of our soul group. An example of this might be a physically or sexually abusive parent. I asked Cameron's angelic guide how this works.

JS: Do we sometimes volunteer to be an antagonist or the bad guy to help each other learn?

Cameron: No.

JS: So how does that work if someone has a lesson that involves an angry father or controlling mother?

Cameron: The attraction comes when someone has a lesson to learn. They will seek out what they need, but no one comes down to be antagonistic to someone. So if someone needs a lesson learned, they will seek that person out that will be of that lesson to them. No one comes in to be antagonistic.

JS: So we come in neutral and then choose an angry father or controlling mother?

Cameron: Or the person that needs the lesson will be drawn to that energy. So, by default, [they] will go to that antagonistic person, but no one agrees to come in to be the antagonist. If someone needs a lesson, they will be attracted to the person who gives them what they need.

Based on similar responses from other guides, it appears that if we need a minor antagonist—for example, someone who rejects us or refuses to commit to a relationship—a member from our soul family might play that role. If there is a need for a more sinister antagonist, the individual learning the lesson will often need to find a person outside of their soul group to be a predator or enemy.

We can be antagonists to other members of our soul family when we incarnate; however, we don't give up our evolutionary standing in order to be a bad person, even if it is to help one of our fellow soul family members. Knowing that we continually build on, and never digress, when it comes to our spiritual growth is certainly an incentive for individuals to do their work and evolve. Felicia, working with four guides, explains that our group members won't sacrifice their consciousness to assist with another being's lesson.

JS: Felicia has become pretty evolved as a human being in this lifetime. Could she come back in the next life as a horrible mother who is verbally and emotionally abusive?

Felicia: She wouldn't do that.

JS: Do you mean she wouldn't agree, and it would it be somebody who's less evolved?

Felicia: Once you gain a certain insight and elevation, then there is an awareness where you would never agree to come back to that, so you could not bring those energies back in. There are many who have the opportunity to do that again and again and again, and our placement here—your book will help, they say—they say that the information that is coming through right now is what will absolutely offer the ability to come into a different place when we are agreeing to such contracts as what you're talking about.

The guides say that Felicia would never let go of her enlightenment to become a hardhearted antagonist for another soul group member. Unfortunately, the guides say that there are many people available who can fill the need for that. The soul member who requires a negative being to further their learning will find and choose a life dynamic where that antagonist exists and incarnate into that dynamic.

Interestingly enough, sometimes within those negative situations, both parties—the soul family member and the harsh antagonist from the outside—have the opportunity to evolve. Certainly, some abusers stay stuck in who they are and never gain any insight, but others can sometimes become repentant. We have all witnessed cases of disagreeable individuals who have undergone dramatic changes after seeing how their harmful behavior has affected those around them. It may take a lifetime of observing how their actions have affected others and often the revelation and the subsequent reversal of demeanor comes too late to repair the damage with the individuals they've wronged, but the transformation suggests that—sometimes—there is the potential for both parties to learn and grow from the situation.

Melanie's guide talks about the dynamic of evolutionary growth and how it has a wide-ranging effect: we not only move with the same group of souls, but the learning or evolution of one soul can impact the entire group because we are all energetically connected and evolving together. Our soul family becomes more enlightened as we become more aware. This communal phenomenon might explain how a family dynamic might change through the years. As one member of that family evolves, many of those around them behave differently.

JS: Do we reincarnate with the same group of people or once we lose someone then we lose them for good?

Melanie: No. No, we're in it for the long haul. We're in it for the long haul and that's why when people do their work, when they do their own internal work energetically, they never have to say a single thing to the people around them because everyone starts to align. Everyone just knows something's changed. Something's changed for all of us because you're connected to everybody, we're all one thing. Everybody's one thing. When there's a change in the one energetically, the rest of us get the benefit of it. Even those who are waiting to come back to us are feeling it. So wherever they are in their chain, they're connected into it as well. They feel that shift.

This takes us back to the energetic connection we all share. The connection we share with those around us is so strong that as one person evolves, the entire group advances. When the guide says that "even those who are waiting to come back to us are feeling it," the implication is that those in our group who are not presently in a physical body benefit as well. My clients often notice as they work on their issues that it can dramatically change the relationships and the dynamics they share with the people around them. Old familial patterns will frequently shift if one of the soul group members undergoes personal growth. It is sometimes hard to remember, but we are all energies interacting with other energies. When one of those beings undergoes personal growth, it affects the dynamic of the entire group.

Knowing that we move through our various existences with the same group of souls should provide comfort in that we don't actually "lose" people when they die. From the human perspective, when someone passes away, that is the end. If you look at it from the Universal perspective, it is a completely different situation: through life and death, we all remain very much connected. This was confirmed by a guide that Amy described as a goddess when I asked about my personal experience.

JS: What about the personal connections we make on this planet, like our friends and families? Are we still connected to those people? Take, for example, my mother. She made her transition years ago. Do I reconnect with her in another lifetime or on another plane?

Amy [interrupting]: You're still connected, right now.

JS: So we stay connected?

Amy: Right now.

JS: All the time.

Amy: Yes.

On many occasions during these sessions, I felt like these concepts were being simplified in an attempt to make them understandable to our human minds. It often appeared as if the guides were trying to help by providing kindergarten explanations to graduate school concepts.

JS: Is it the same small group of people or energies that we keep working with on every plane?

Amy: Yes, you travel in groups, but it's such a limited way of seeing it because you're connected to all that is. You're connected to everything.

JS: What if someone becomes very evolved in this lifetime? Do they move on or graduate to another group of people? Do they lose touch with the people who are not as evolved? Or is this just the human mind trying to make sense of these things?

Amy: Everyone is working toward ascension at different speeds. Everyone has their own pace. The energies are always connected even as the frequencies change. So, even though they may fall away from you in this life—people will fall away from you—the energy is still there. The heart connection is still there.

JS: So when you say my mother is still with me now, what does that look like? Are we working together on other planes?

Amy: You are working together on other planes, but on this plane you feel their energy envelop you, offering assistance, checking in on you. You can call on her when you need her. That particular spark of her is still with you, guiding you. And yet at the same time, you are working together in other places, other dimensions, on a closer level.

JS: Are you saying that our spirits can go in so many directions that she can be here and she can be in all of these other places at the same time?

Amy: Yes.

JS: And I can as well?

Amy: And you are.

Amy's guide says that not only do we maintain a connection with those who have departed in this life, but we are actively working with them on other dimensions as well. This further reinforces the idea that we are multidimensional beings working on multiple planes. To the human mind, we see the dynamics after transition as a linear event. In other words, we believe—and have been told—that we go in one direction. For example, we were told we go to heaven *or* we reincarnate and come back to Earth in another body *or* we become a guide to our children and grandchildren, and so on, but the insight from our guides is that we might be doing all of those things and a whole lot more. If we go back to the amoeba example, we have hundreds of spiritual tentacles that are experiencing multiple dimensions all at once.

These insights about our ongoing connection to "energies" from our soul group give us the opportunity to alter our views regarding the end of human life. Based on the information from the guides in Chapter 2, our perception of the finality of death is based on an erroneous manmade paradigm. If we had a deep knowing that we don't really "lose" these beings around us when a death occurs, and we all continue to remain connected, it would be easier to process transitions. But most of our earthly views about death focus on finality. In our vocabulary, we use phrases such as "final resting place," "I'm sorry about your loss," and "no longer with us." It is rare to hear someone express a perspective where death is no more than a brief separation on this earthly plane and we'll be together with that loved one for many, many lifetimes.

To illustrate how we remain bonded to people who are close to us, as I asked questions about soul families, Danielle became aware of the presence of someone with her.

JS: While we're here, we make strong connections to other people on this planet: friends, family members, etc. Do we continue to move through these different planes with them? Do we stay together as a group, or do we only once experience someone's energy and that's it?

Danielle: This is very easy. They're our soul family. Some choose to come here with us at certain times for short intervals. Some choose to stay with us and teach us. They may be good, they may be bad to our physical, but they're still with us. So my grandmother came when you are saying that because she is a prime example. This is my first life without her here, so she stands beside me, protects me, and guides me and lives this life through me until I can be with her again. That is the example.

The "example" of Danielle's grandmother illustrates how strong our connection is to people in our soul family. Danielle's grandmother is not on the earthly plane, but she appeared as soon as Danielle asked for guidance. We are not abandoned when one of our soul group members makes their transition.

> JS: Since she [Danielle's grandmother] is part of your soul family, you will continue to evolve together and be together on different planes; is that right?
>
> Danielle: Um-hm. She says that we still work together, and that she just does it from over there. And, yes, as a soul family we do evolve together.

There is no separation in death: we are still very much connected, and the members of each soul family are evolving together.

The opening question of this chapter was: Do we stay connected to those who are close to us? It's always hard to put a number or percentage on the consistency of the answers from the guides. The answer to this question was generally a consensus. After asking this question hundreds of times, I would say that at least 98 percent of the guides echoed the same sentiments: we are very connected to our soul families. The variance in this answer is probably twofold. One, there is the occasional soul who comes into our group for a specific purpose and then moves on. The other variance might be that we can go to other dimensions and choose to stay off of the Earth for a few lifetimes. That doesn't mean we've abandoned our soul family, it just means our learning or our journey can temporarily take us somewhere else.

There would be much less fear around death if we accepted that death isn't the end and we knew in our hearts that we maintain our personal connections.

So, based on what the guides have told us, will I ever see the elders from my family with whom I shared time on that summer evening? Of course. Not only were they there then, but they are probably with me now, helping to guide me as I write this. Instead of feeling loss, I should be looking forward to how we will meet again and continue to evolve together.

And what was the message of that age regression session in which I was enjoying a summer picnic with my elders? I thought about it when the session was over, and after a while, it came to me. That one moment was very precious. As a child, I had no idea that it was the end of the tribe—on the earthly plane. It felt like we would be together forever. In my body, I felt very alive and didn't give a single thought to anything but being there and feeling that connection. And that was a part of the learning. I was there and *in the moment*. If I had been preoccupied with something from the past or worried about how things might take shape in the future, I would have missed the teachings that, on some level, I absorbed on that summer evening. So, the guidance was to embrace the moment and be present.

Our spiritual lessons are being presented to us on an ongoing basis, and it is our responsibility to be present so we can receive that information; unfortunately, we live in a world of distractions and few of us are actively open to the messages directed our way. If we aren't paying attention, we can easily miss the guidance that is available to us. This topic is something the guides address again in Chapter 10.

In conclusion, one of my clients, who was being shown images by her guide, described the notion of soul families and how closely connected we are to other members of our soul family by using an artistic metaphor to capture the concept.

*Imagine a weaving of threads, different colored threads. It's a perfectly symmetrical design, and there are lots of threads that intersect in a pattern as they touch each other. Now turn them into light. These light threads are together forever. They represent the lives and multiple lives of those in our family: we can call them "beloveds." They are our family forever, and they always have been.*

The image of "threads" or cords of light comes up again in Chapter 9, which explores the concept of time. Each of us—as threads of light—"are together forever" with the people who are close to us. We have become accustomed to regarding transitions as losses, but in the grander picture, the guides want us to know that we are intricately interwoven, and "they are our family forever, and they always have been."

# Chapter 5
# Are Our Lives Predetermined?

In my 20s, when I was living just outside of Los Angeles, I had an experience that changed my life. I was driving up the coastline to the Santa Barbara area on one of those rare occasions when Southern California was getting pounded by a powerful rainstorm. The storm was ominous enough that, during the day, the local news stations were warning people to stay home if they didn't need to go out that night, a caution that was rarely given in a place known for temperate weather.

It was an especially dark night because the thick, low clouds obscured most of the city lights. Because the streets and highways in Southern California weren't designed to handle substantial rainfall, the water was pooling and collecting wherever there were low spots in the road. As I drove along Highway 101, there were several times when the pavement would drop down into a dip or depression that had filled with water and the car would hydroplane, completely losing contact with the ground. I remember, at one point, wondering if that hydroplaning might actually pull the car across the median and into the oncoming traffic.

When I turned off of the main highway and started driving on side roads it was a bit of a relief, but it was still very dark and hard to see as the rain continued to fall. I was trying to be very cautious, but not everyone adjusts to the conditions. Suddenly, an SUV coming from the other direction lost control and came into my lane. That vehicle, at least twice the size and weight of the car I was driving, was headed straight toward me.

In that instant, I had two choices: absorb the head-on impact or try to avoid contact by swerving out of the way and running up a steep bank on the side of the road that most likely would flip the car. In either case, the outcome would be catastrophic.

It happened so fast that there was no time to think. I tried to steer the car somewhere between the oncoming SUV and the grassy bank. The result was still a head-on collision, but the last-minute maneuver slightly lessened the force of the crash. I was knocked unconscious by the impact and pulled from the car by witnesses who were afraid the car was going to go up in flames. Fortunately, I was able to fully recover from the accident, but at the time, I was beat up from the impact, and for several weeks I had headaches from the concussion.

In those weeks after the accident, I couldn't make sense of why I needed to go through that pain and trauma. Instead of taking time to convalesce, I immediately went back to work, trying to push through the pain. That was how I was raised: work came first. I didn't know any better.

I had a very demanding job where I was working about 60 hours a week, and I soon discovered it was too much to go back to that work while dealing with the aftereffects of a concussion. That was the beginning of the end of that career, and not long after that I ended up giving my notice.

When a traumatic event like that happens, it brings up a lot of emotions. Certainly there was anger at the other driver. There was anger at my workplace, where there seemed to be a lack of empathy. There was sadness, loneliness, and despondency. There was a great deal of questioning about why the accident needed to happen. I even wondered if I was being punished for something I had done in the past. None of it made sense. There was no reason or logic to help me understand what I gone through.

Years later, when I looked back at that incident hoping to find clarity, I finally felt like I was able to make sense of what happened. The way I saw it was that I was in a corporate job that was stealing the life out me. I was making good money, but I was also giving away all of my time and energy to a career that was completely wrong for me. So, in that retrospective moment, I determined that the accident was the Universe stepping in and changing my life direction. I wasn't meant to be doing that corporate job, and what occurred on that stormy night was a deliberate plan to get me away from that diversion and get my life back on track.

If it wasn't for the accident, I might've stayed in that profession. After I left that job, I had the opportunity to refocus on what I wanted my life to become. A small settlement from the accident gave me enough money to go back to school and earn a teaching credential, which eventually led me to teach and work with students. Teaching felt much more in line with what I was supposed to be doing during my time here on the planet, so I attributed that event, even though it was a painful one, to Divine intervention.

For many years, I accepted that explanation. I was convinced that the Universe had stepped in and changed the course of my life. It was one of those instances when I felt hindsight was able to provide clarity.

However, as I grew spiritually, I began to wonder if the Universe really does step in and alter the course of our lives. Is the Universe running the show or am I in charge of the direction of my life? As I learned more about spiritual teachings, such as the law of attraction— where we can manifest what we want to create in our lives through our thoughts, actions, and words—it appeared that we, through our free will, are in control of what our lives look like.

But those two beliefs contradict one another. In one scenario, we create our own lives and what happens to us. In the other, the Universe is an active participant and there is an element of fate or predetermination in our lives. Which one is the real truth? Is the Universe directing everything that happens to us or is our destiny completely of our own making? I needed to know, so I asked the guides: are our lives predetermined or do we have free will to create the lives we choose?

As I began conversations on this subject, I started with the big picture: do we come onto this planet with a general plan or outline of how our lives are supposed to unfold, or is everything improvised? I asked Beatrice's guide, a close friend who had made her transition and come back as a guide, if we have the ability to be a co-creator of our life.

JS: Are we a co-creator of our existence or is there a destiny that we are following? Are we responsible for how our life unfolds or is it prewritten?

Beatrice: It's a bit of both. Your destiny isn't prewritten, but there is an overall outline of how things could end up, and through a series of choices and questions because as you question things, new things pop up. And you start to go down different paths, and then when you go down a different path, another set of questions may arise. And depending on the answers that you find, you may go down another path as well. To say that everything is set in stone takes away the freedom of discovery, and that the freedom of discovery is where the essence comes in and the growth takes place. You can't necessarily have that if everything is predestined.

The answer to the matter of whether we have a predestined life or a life we where we can exert our influence appears to be "a bit of both." We do have a framework or "outline" in which we operate, but we are able to make "choices," and those choices open us to different pathways that can lead us in a variety of directions. Our growth comes from "discovery." "Freedom of discovery" appears to be another way of describing our learning process. If everything was prewritten, we wouldn't be able to choose and discover, and it is those abilities that enable us to learn and evolve.

If we are here to grow and discover, it seems only logical that there would need to be some sort of life blueprint or "overall outline" that would expose us to things that might help facilitate that learning. I asked Caroline's guide, an angelic guide, how we choose that master plan.

> JS: How do we choose what our life is going to look like? What does that process look like?

> Caroline: It's a soul consciousness that says there's an agreement that your soul makes to heal things from your past soul lives, and we don't really know exactly what the method will be, but there's an agreement or desire—it's really truly a desire— that the soul has to let go and surrender even more to the opportunity in the next life to learn and grow.

The idea that we are here to "learn and grow" was a common theme with the guides. Our existence on this planet is *not* random. We make agreements where our objective is to "heal things from past soul lives." In other words, we incarnate with things to work on and, in order to facilitate that process, it appears that we attract certain conflicts and situations related to our learning.

When Caroline's guide speaks of healing things from "past soul lives," it sounds like how the guides describe karma. I talk about karma in Chapter 6. In this case, the essential element of karma is about focusing on whatever lessons we need to address as part of our personal evolution. It isn't about karma as punishment or payback; instead, it is about what events and situations can facilitate the learning that the soul needs in order to grow. I asked Carolyn's angelic guide how we choose our life plan and how much free will we have once we come into being.

JS: Do you choose your life based on what will further your path and your learning?

Caroline: Um-hm. Yeah.

JS: Does that include choosing parents and situations?

Caroline: Absolutely.

JS: And when we get here, when we incarnate and become a human, are things pretty much predetermined in our lives or do we have free will and can go in different directions?

Caroline: We have lots of opportunity and choices, and that's what the whole experience is about. You choose your lesson in a sense, but your path is open and that's where you can have fun in life and even though you may choose to heal a victim standpoint, let's say, you can choose situations that minimize or heal pain. So you don't have to go through horrible things in order to live out your lesson that you came to do. Some people choose it the other way. Some people don't choose at all and then it can get a little punky.

The angelic guide says that we choose a path or outline, but once we begin our existence in a human body, it is up to us to determine how our lives will take shape. The words *free will* came up often in discussions on this topic. Even though there is a basic plan we choose to incarnate with, we have the power to mold or shape our lives. There is no predeterminism or fatalism, those belief systems that dictate that all life events are predetermined and inevitable; instead, we have the capability to influence our own lives.

Caroline's guide also said that we sign up for lessons, but that learning can be difficult or easy based on the work we do along the way. I believe, in this context, when the guide mentioned people who "don't choose at all," she was referring to those individuals who decide to ignore their lessons while they are here on the planet.

Their lives can get "punky" in that they might spend their entire life living with anger or depression, or a repetition of painful events or relationships where familiar patterns—patterns that might go back several incarnations—continue to repeat. The master plan appears to be that our learning is a part of our evolution, so if we choose to ignore those lessons, those teachings will keep coming back in slightly different forms with different casts of characters.

It is important to talk about what is meant by the word *lesson*, as that term is used often in this book, and it can sometimes feel like a loaded word with negative connotations. For example, sometimes learning a lesson can conjure up memories of being *taught* a lesson, which sounds and feels like a punishment. We must remember, however, that based on the responses in Chapter 1, the Divine is not punishing or vengeful; it is loving and forgiving. And it is important to clarify that the Divine is *not* choosing our lessons, we are. Our master life plan is something *we* choose as a means to move forward in our evolution. No one is forcing these lessons upon us. Each of us has agreed to a life outline which contains these challenges that serve to enable us to grow.

If the word *lesson* has negative connotations for you, there are several other words that can be substituted or used to describe the dynamic of facing challenges that help us grow. Other descriptors that might feel less weighted include *awareness* or *understanding* or *discovering our purpose*. It is perfectly okay for readers to insert those other expressions whenever the word lesson is used as long as we don't lose sight of the purpose of those challenging experiences and their role in helping us to grow.

Although the great majority of the guides talked about life plans or outlines, most were quick to bring up free will. Our free will can trump the life plan. We come in with a general game plan, but once we hit the ground we can play it by ear. We have a program outline when we are born, but, if we choose, we can throw out that program and never look at it again, thus allowing free will to be the only compass to direct our lives. The conversation with Source, through Brett, explains how this works.

JS: Is there a planned agenda for each of us when we come onto this planet? For example, Brett is going to come here, he's going to marry, he's going to have two children, he's going to paint with watercolors, and he'll get into the field of computer technology. Is this predetermined or is this all about free will?

Brett: It often depends upon the level of development in each soul. Some souls will plan a very specific role for themselves. Others play it by ear; they really have no set agenda. Free will plays a big role in it. You can set an agenda and still alter it once you come into that incarnation. Free will trumps everything. Sometimes that can be good and sometimes that can be bad. People who are very unhappy, often it is because they made a free will decision to circumvent their design, their intentions. Other people stay with the same intentions and they never really get out of it, so they actually do need to change their course. That's how a warrior becomes a pacifist. He can't stay in that warrior mode for every incarnation, even if that's his intention.

In this dialogue, the implication is that people can become "very unhappy" when they ignore their plan, and because of free will, everyone has the potential to do that. Perhaps that unhappiness manifests as depression in those individuals who don't face their lessons or adhere to their life plan. Conversely, it sounds like the more evolved the soul, the stronger the agenda. Perhaps that is why there are individuals on this planet who seem to be driven, whereas others can be directionless.

The warrior example might illustrate how a lesson could unfold. If the warrior's objective is to find and experience a peaceful existence, he can ignore that lesson for several incarnations. As he does this, he might eventually feel a sense of alienation from his purpose, causing him to develop more anger, which, in turn, might feed the aggressive warrior persona. That might continue through many lifetimes until something happens—perhaps he chooses a lifetime blueprint in which he loses someone very close to him as a result of a violent encounter—and that affects him deeply on a soul level. Because of that event, a shift occurs and he becomes able to embrace his mission and transform into a pacifist.

Based on multiple conversations on this topic, only a handful of which were presented here, it appears that each of us agrees to a basic blueprint that might include characteristics of people in our lives and general situations and events that will occur. For example, we might choose parents who withhold love in order for us to learn to love ourselves. We might choose a dynamic in which we can become greedy in order to learn that happiness does not come from money. We might choose a career where we give up our identity in order to discover that we feel empty inside and need to break away from that oppressive employer and step into our power. Initially, we agree to those general dynamics, but once we are here, we have free will. Our free will can guide us to embrace what our soul wants us to discover, but, conversely, our free will can lead us in other directions. For example, that soul with parents who withhold love might decide that their parents were correct and he or she goes through their entire life feeling not worthy. That greedy individual might choose to cling to their money even though they end up dying sad and alone. The person who gives up their individuality may never resign from the demeaning corporate job and never emerge as the leader they envisioned when they selected their life plan. Once we are here, on this planet, free will comes into play. Nothing about the blueprint is set in stone. It is simply an outline that we can embrace or ignore. And, it appears, that we don't always pay attention to our purpose or figure things out in a single incarnation. People often say that if you don't figure it out this time, you can come back and do it all over again. To some degree, that may be true.

So, if we start with a general outline, how much influence do we really have in terms of manifesting what we want to create in our lives? Can we use the law of attraction—a process by which we manifest things we want to create in life through our thoughts, feelings, and beliefs—to create a vastly different life from the outline we incarnated with?

I asked Beatrice's guide what happens when we move away from our path.

> JS: If something comes up, for example, Beatrice decides she wants to move to New York, but the Universe feels like the move to New York might not be good for her. She is better here in Colorado, and if she goes to New York she might really struggle. How much can or does the Universe impact or influence those decisions?

I picked New York because Beatrice had, in the past, been drawn to the lure of big cities, only to discover that it wasn't a good fit for her.

> Beatrice: The Universe supports everything. And the Universe, to be fair, is not just running its own show. It's also running on who they're programming it with.

The Universe is *not* "running its own show." We are the ultimate programmer of our lives. If we start moving in the wrong direction, the Universe can simply make one path easier than another by creating blocks or obstacles when we make choices that don't serve our highest good.

> Beatrice: It can intervene in different ways. One soft option would be to open up a lot of opportunities in that city were the Universe wants you to stay. Another would be, if you're hell bent on going to New York, allowing you to go to New York and making you so uncomfortable that your only option is to come back immediately, or within a few months. But that's usually for those that are efforting people.

"Efforting people," refers to those people who push against the flow of life. Instead of following the signs, some individuals will ignore their path—and ignore the flow—and try to force their own agenda to work.

> Beatrice: You don't have to effort. There's no pulling strings. There is no manipulating. There's no trying to convince people. It just happens. It really does happen that fluidly when you are in the flow and in the trust, and you're following the path that you are supposed to be on, things start to align. It's when we start to effort, and we go away from that. No, that's not the result I wanted, so I'm going to force myself over here, and then you go over here and there's so many things, not just the tactical things from day-to-day, you're empty inside, you don't feel connected, disease may pop up, anxiety, depression, because anxiety and depression are mere symptoms of being off your path, and the more acute your anxiety or your depression is telling how far off your path you are.

The message is to pay attention to the signs around you. It feels very different when everything falls in place, as opposed to trying to force the results one wants to create. We have free will to do what we choose, but if we drift away from our path, there will be something inside that might feel empty or disconnected. Sometimes getting away from our path could lead to "anxiety," "depression," or even "disease" because our essence is disconnected from Divine energy and our chosen plan. In a sense, that disconnected soul is ailing because it is experiencing a sense of alienation as it has lost its way.

What about the original question, regarding whether or not Beatrice could beat the system and use the law of attraction and go to New York? She could do that, but the Universe might make it feel uncomfortable and might not open any opportunistic doors for her if it takes her away from her true purpose. Everyone in this day and age wants to embrace the law of attraction, but if the desire is not aligned with a soul's purpose, it appears that the desired outcome may not take place.

That brings up yet another question of how much influence can the Universe, or our guides, impose when we attempt to move in a direction that takes us away from our path. Sylvia's animal guide addressed that question.

JS: What if we come onto this planet and we start going in the wrong direction in terms of our evolution? In other words, if somebody is growing and becoming more spiritual and able to help a lot of people, and then they turn and go down the wrong path, do they get nudged? Do their guides or angels help put them back in place, or is it free will or they can do what they want?

Sylvia: There are guides that are with them that will give them an opportunity to see. No guide would ever force someone to see. It is impossible, but they would give them opportunity, multiple opportunities, to continue to choose differently. There is a mass consciousness that also is a part of the planet and people will bump into it. Some people rail against it. Some people see a glimmer. Some people stand and hold the grid of that energy. There's always an opportunity for someone to see something and make a choice that moves in a different direction for themselves.

JS: So they may see something that looks more positive if they choose a different direction, or maybe they'll find doors closing that prevent them from going in the wrong direction as indicators?

Sylvia: A vibration may come along or could come along, that they don't know why but feel comfortable with it. That may guide them in a different, more helpful direction.

In one of the earlier passages, one of the guides mentioned "soft options." That might be the best way to describe how our guides or inner guidance manages situations when we have chosen the wrong path or are trying to manifest outcomes that don't align with our highest good. The guides can't "force someone to see," but they can make one path more comfortable than another.

We have talked about the two divergent paths: individuals who follow their blueprint and people who completely ignore their life plan. It is important to acknowledge that, most likely, a large part of the population falls somewhere between those two extremes. They may not follow their exact blueprint, but they address parts of it and still learn and have a productive life. Perhaps they aren't zeroed in on learning every lesson, but they are tackling some of the challenges that can help them evolve.

Often, there can be multiple ways to approach that desired learning. There might be several options that lead to the same outcome. For example, someone who is here to help people heal may do that as an actual healer, but there can be many other paths that foster that goal. They might be a supportive companion to a dying friend in that friend's time of need. They might be a teacher who heals by providing a safe environment for children to learn without judgment or fear. They might heal by creating watercolors of scenes that help disillusioned people reach a state of inner peace as they momentarily escape through that art. There are many ways to achieve the desired outcome, and the journey doesn't always take the shape we expect.

Maya's male spirit guide talks about how there can be multiple paths leading to a desired outcome after encapsulating much of what has been expressed in this chapter.

JS: When we come onto this planet, do we choose things like our parents and our lessons?

Maya [interrupting]: Yes and yes. He [referring to her guide] answers before you finish talking.

During these sessions, clients would often tell me that their guides would answer questions before I had finished asking the questions. Some clients added that guides would occasionally become impatient, as if they already knew what I was going to ask and they wanted to start answering before I was done talking.

JS: When we get here, do we *have* to follow that plan or is it about free will?

Maya: No. You don't have to follow it.

JS: And if we don't, what happens?

Maya: You work it out in another way.

JS: You learn it another way?

Maya: Um-hm.

JS: If we go in the wrong direction, say Maya has a plan to help people through teaching, but instead she decides I am going to quit teaching and I'm going to...

Maya [interrupting]: She'll find another way. Another way will be thrust upon her.

We often want to be in charge of how things might manifest in our lives, but apparently, there are a variety of paths that can lead us to where we need to go. Additionally, a lesson might come together through multiple existences as in the warrior/pacifist example.

JS: We have the law of attraction here, which is what you think and feel and believe is what you create. Say Maya wants to become a millionaire; can she do that with free will and the law of attraction?

Maya: She could try, but there is a certain path you still have to take, one way or another. It's almost like one of those puzzles that you find your way through the maze to the center. There are a lot of ways to get to the center, but you will have to make your way to that center, that objective. You can try different paths, but they're all going to end up steering you towards what you're supposed to be doing.

The analogy of a maze, with the finish in the center, and with several different paths that lead to that end result is very fitting because there are many ways to reach our desired outcomes. Perhaps Maya stops teaching, makes millions in the stock market, and then spends the remainder of her life engaged in philanthropy; she may have still found the perfect end point. It is about her lesson, and there isn't always a single path to realize that lesson. What might look like a misstep to the human mind may not be, because we often don't know the nature of the lesson Maya, or any of us, is here to learn.

Earlier in this chapter, the topic of "soft options" our guides might use to nudge us in the proper direction was discussed. Can the Universe create hard options as well? If I go back to that auto accident I experienced, that didn't feel like a soft option. Can the Universe take more extreme measures to keep us on our path? I wanted to know, so I asked Chelsea's goddess guide more specific questions relating to that event.

JS: I was in a severe car accident in my 20s, and years later I looked at it as something that happened to get me to change the path I was on. Is that how it works?

Chelsea: Yes. That's your oversoul, not the Universe. That's your oversoul, shaking things up, helping you evolve.

This clarification is important. The Universe didn't create the accident, nor did my guides. It was my oversoul that interrupted things.

JS: Interesting. So it's not the Universe doing that, it's really a part of me when you say the oversoul. Something in me said that this is the wrong path, stop this, and change directions.

Chelsea: Yes.

JS: Tell me more about the oversoul.

Chelsea: The oversoul is your spark, your beam from the creator, your ray, your conductor, conducting the orchestra of all your different beings in different existences.

It is interesting that without prompting from me, Chelsea's guide refers to multiple existences.

> JS: So, if we're on the wrong path, it is more likely our oversoul would see something and do something or nudge us in some way, but maybe with the help of a spirit guide or something. So the oversoul might go to the spirit guide and say give him a little nudge or open this door for him.
>
> Chelsea: Yes.

According to Chelsea's spirit guide, this was not the Universe taking action; it was my oversoul. The oversoul might be compared to the central nervous system of that amoeba we talked about in Chapter 3, the amoeba with all the tentacles that are actively experiencing multiple incarnations. Something inside of me, on a soul level, orchestrated that accident to move me back to my original life plan. It wasn't my guides or angels or the Universe; apparently, it was something I instigated.

Seeking confirmation in regards to my choosing that traumatic event, I asked Janet's praying mantis guide about the event.

> JS: I had a severe accident that changed the course of where my life was going. I felt like I was going in the wrong direction. Do we manifest something like a car accident to get us to change directions?
>
> Janet: You asked for that, ahead of time, to keep you on your path. You may leave if you choose [decide] it's too hard. You chose to stay then.

Apparently, I could have made my transition and left the planet at that point in my life. That car accident was a potential exit point. I chose to stay, and, on some level, some part of my being had asked—possibly in advance as part of my life plan—for a wake-up call if I deviated from my path.

JS: So I had asked, at some point in time, to help me right the ship?

Janet: Um-hm.

JS: What if we want to manifest [something in our lives], can we do that?

Janet: This is easy. There is no time. We wish, ask, beg, and plead for things we desire, not knowing that the reason is because what we want and desire is ahead of us, and somehow we already yearn to get to that point. It is our script. Some things we know deep down inside, but don't understand.

JS: I'm not sure I understand. Can you explain that in a different way?

Janet: Your life is a script. You know the end before you come. I do not call them manifestations. Your desires, your wants, they are something you know is coming that you don't understand yet. Somehow, deep inside you, you know it.

It sounds like, on a higher level, we already know the end of "the script" or end point of the maze. We know what we want to accomplish in life. We are aware of how the script is supposed to end. In a sense, that knowing is already imprinted in our minds. When we try to manifest things that correspond with that end point, we are able to create what we desire. If we are trying to manifest things that conflict with that endpoint, we are unlikely to be successful. Apparently, I wanted so much to reach my desired end point that I was willing to undergo a serious car crash to keep me on course.

Could it have been done in another way? If I hadn't undergone that experience, I would not be where I am today. If it had been more subtle, perhaps the lesson may not have been fully received. That event shaped who I am. Without it, perhaps the healing work—and perhaps this book—may have never come to fruition. In some way, part of my agreement was to undergo a hard option if I strayed too far from my path.

If we go back to the initial question of whether or not our lives are predetermined, here is the wisdom of the guides. We all come into this incarnation with lessons to learn that will assist us in our personal evolution. We agree to a basic outline of what our lessons are and a life dynamic that provides us opportunities to learn those lessons. Even though we have a general life outline, it is no more than that: an outline. We can choose to follow it or not follow it, and we can even change our direction as life progresses. We all have free will. Our lives are not predestined. If we choose to ignore our path, we may experience negative feelings such as anger, depression, separation, and anxiety. If we follow our blueprint, there is a sense of flow where things fall in place easily for us. If we try to manifest things that are not in alignment with our higher purpose, then, as one guide put it, "They simply will not happen." There can be multiple paths that take us to that desired endpoint of learning that is consistent with our agreement. It is like a maze in which several routes can lead to the finish line. Our guides might help direct us, but they cannot and will not interfere with our journey. That guidance might be as simple as finding a lack of opportunities when we choose the wrong direction and discovering open doors when we pursue a destiny that is aligned with our purpose.

On a soul level, we can ask for intervention—a wake-up call—but this is orchestrated by our oversoul and is not the result of an intrusive Universe or guides or angels that have overstepped their bounds. We can ask for it—as I apparently did years ago—and perhaps without it, this book would never have come into being.

## Chapter 6

# Is There Such a Thing as Karma?

The first time I experienced a past life regression was with the late author and hypnotist Bryan Jameison. At the time of that regression, I had no idea that I would end up working with hypnotherapy as a career as the session occurred several years before I entered this profession. I was intrigued by the idea of learning about how we may have been here before, and I was interested to know if some of the events in my current lifetime might be connected to past lives. I was seeking clarity and closure and maybe even a logical understanding about issues and experiences I had been facing on this earthly plane.

One of the questions I had was about someone in my life whose behavior could best be described as antagonistic and narcissistic. I admit that, at that time, I didn't know all that much about relationship dynamics. I understood that I was a participant in the dysfunction and had some responsibility for the conflict, but I didn't understand why this individual, by all appearances, wanted to take everything from me. There was no logical explanation and no event or occurrence in our current life to justify that behavior.

So, I wanted to see if there was some sort of past life event that might shed light on this relationship dynamic. Maybe there was something that occurred in a previous life that would explain everything.

When we broached that question in hypnosis, I quickly regressed to a past life where I was about to face off in a duel with that same individual with whom I was having issues in this lifetime. Naturally, each of us was in a different physical body at that time, but it was clear that we were the same two individuals who were having differences in our present existence.

The setting appeared to be some time in the late 1700s or early 1800s, and the weapons we had chosen were pistols. The rules of the duel were simple. After selecting our weapons, we were instructed to stand back-to-back and wait for the confrontation to begin. We were each to take 10 paces, as the official counted down from 10 to one, and on the count of one, we were to turn and shoot.

As the official called out each number, we somberly took our steps in opposite directions. When the count got down to about three, I turned and fired my pistol. My adversary went down with a fatal gunshot wound, and though it may not have been my proudest moment, I lived to see another day.

From this event, it seemed clear that this person in my current life who seemed so self-absorbed and wanted to take whatever they could was simply coming from a place of retribution. This was karma as I understood it. I had done them wrong and now they were settling the score.

At the time of that age regression session, I believed in karma so it all made sense: do something in one life and you pay for it in another. The concept of karma seemed just; although, for some people in this world, it didn't seem to occur as rapidly as I would've liked.

Based on that regression, by all appearances, karma truly existed. Having an acceptance of this concept might be a way to help us walk away from people who have wronged us. We could either assume we had treated that person poorly in another incarnation and this was payback, or we could know that there would eventually be consequences for any of their current wrongdoings. In the latter case, we could much more easily walk away from any situation by saying to ourselves, "Just wait until your karma catches up with you."

I have always wanted to know more about karma. It is often mentioned in spiritual readings in which a client might be told that something from a past life is affecting their journey in this life. But is that really how karma works, or is this a concept that humans created in order to help us walk away from our conflicts?

When I first started asking questions about karma, I was a bit surprised by the answers. Sondra was working with a master, which is a very advanced spirit guide. As I asked for information about karma, her master guide would take her to scenes where she could assimilate answers from what she observed.

JS: Is there such a thing as karma?

Sondra: They're [referring to her guides] trying to talk in my ear. He [her master guide] keeps saying karma, karma, karma. And as he says it, he actually vibrates me back to another life so I could feel the karma. He makes me feel like that would be punishment. [She pauses and takes in the information.] There can't be punishment, he says.

I asked the question in a different way, but Sondra's master guide confirmed.

Sondra: Once we pass, that life is over.

JS: We don't pay for that in another life?

Sondra: No. And I'm kind of shocked I guess.

Usually, after a session, a client would talk to me about how they disagreed with some of the answers provided by their guides. In this case, Sondra expressed her surprise during the session. After getting more information from her guide, she went on to follow up with a metaphorical statement from her master:

Sondra: Once you take that coat off, you leave it here.

Taking off the coat brings us back to the acting analogy. We step into a character for one performance or one lifetime and when we move to another incarnation, we put on a new costume—or coat—and enter a whole different production. In other words, there is no karmic carryover in terms of punishment or retribution.

Roger was working with a spirit animal when I asked him about karma and the notion that we can be punished or, at the very least, be held accountable for our actions.

JS: What about the person on the planet who does bad things that end up hurting people, is there karma? Do they die and get punished in another realm?

Roger: Man-made.

JS: So there is no karma when you die?

Roger: No. It's random. Just whirls of energy. We pass through them. What they do here doesn't matter in other places. Like sticking your finger in a flame, only your one finger gets burned. The other fingers don't matter. The pain you cause here is transitory, but you still shouldn't do it.

Roger's guide, adhering to the multiple dimensions concept, says that what we do here doesn't affect what happens in those other existences. My first thought was that this couldn't be right. Most of us believe in karma, and it has been used by spiritual readers for hundreds of years to help us make sense of actions and events that don't seem to be motivated by logic or normal human behavior. How could the guides be taking this concept away from us?

Jason, working with Source, reinforced the assertion that our long-standing perspective of karma is incorrect because it is based on a premise that there has to be a determination of what is right or wrong, and the Universe is not a place of judgment.

JS: Is there karma for people who come and do things that we label as bad?

Jason: No.

JS: Why not?

Jason: We're letting go of the concept of karma. In the past, the concept of karma has been connected with physics, and in physics you do one action and then there is an equal and opposite reaction. In order to understand that, that's externalized. The connection with karma is externalized because you have to rely on an external contact being, God/Goddess, to tell you whether you're right, wrong, or on track or not on track. A new way of looking at karma would be to connect that with ourselves and our doing.

Once again, karma is dismissed because it would necessitate an evaluation by an external force or being, "God/Goddess," to determine what is right and what is wrong and then inflict appropriate punishment. The guides say that the Divine is a loving and forgiving energy. There is no judgment. On the spirit level, we are loved unconditionally.

In our society, we want to embrace the concept of karma because it falls in line with a simple law of physics: for every action there is an equal and opposite reaction. But that is trying to explain the Universe by using a scientific model. The Universe is not ruled by science. Divine energy is the embodiment of pure unconditional love and forgiveness. How could karma, which is based on judgment and punishment, be associated with Divine energy? That would be a complete contradiction.

As the conversation with Jason continued, Source went on to say that instead of being judged and punished by an external force, any semblance of karma might be more of an internal experience.

Jason: So what we're learning is to take responsibility for our own energy and being and not externalizing that, not putting those thoughts or that energy to anything outside of ourselves. Are there laws of balance? Are there laws of how energy flows? Yes, those are not absolute. If you're in one dimension, they work one way. If you're in another dimension, they work another way. If you're experiencing in one fractal, they work one way. If those laws are in another fractal, they might work another way.

We've been told by numerous guides that the Divine is an energy that is present within all of us and not a judgmental or punishing force. This excerpt suggests that instead of looking at karma as retribution, it may actually be an internal process where we "take responsibility for our own energy and being and not externalizing that, not putting those thoughts or that energy to anything outside of ourselves." Simply put, we must take responsibility for all of our actions and not rely on some universal payback system to teach us what is right or wrong and, subsequently, even the score. Personal evolution is an internal process that involves aligning with the consciousness of the Universe. The drive to evolve must come voluntarily from deep within one's being: it is not designed to be motivated by payback or punishment.

Kelsey, also working with Source, elaborated on how karma might be more about internal unrest and not an external payback system.

JS: What about karma? We're all here making mistakes, and the human belief is if you do something wrong, you're going to pay for it in the next life or the afterlife. What does Source say about karma?

Kelsey: Consequences are only an element of our physical being. If we do something, hurt someone, we pay for that in this life. Nobody really gets away with anything. In the next life, it's like turning the chapter in a book. You go on to the next chapter. You can review those things. You can feel, perhaps, how you hurt people, and that can be an unpleasant experience, but there's no payback. There's no retribution. There's no coming back as a bug because you were bad. That's a very human, very physical mindset. We feel that if you do A, you have to have B. You have to suffer, be punished in some way. But that's not the way it works. The evil we do in our lives, the bad things we do, are a result of our separation, our fear, and once we pass out of this form we lose all of that. We lose all that fear, and so there would be no point in the consequences.

Again, we are told that the notion of a retaliatory system of karma is a "human, very physical mindset," and the real consequence may be an "unpleasant" internal experience. That internal experience is probably what is supposed to help us grasp our lessons. Some people feel bad and begin to change, whereas others are able to ignore what they feel inside and subsequently ignore their lessons. There isn't payback or retribution, but the wrongdoer might experience some internal strife, in this lifetime, about what they did. Kelsey goes on to talk about those inner repercussions:

Kelsey: But that's not to say that we don't suffer as a result of these things, but we suffer in different ways in our own life. We might suffer in the respect that we're so arrogant that we have no friends, and we spend the last years of our lives alone. We might suffer in a way that we never have a moment of peace even though we have tremendous wealth, like a drug kingpin. He's got a mansion, he's got millions of dollars, yet he can't enjoy a moment of it because he knows someone is going to try to take it from him or probably kill him or his family. So, our karma is experienced within this lifetime, and sometimes it can be a horrific experience, but when we come into this incarnation we're not bringing any of this from the past with us.

The internal unrest, within the offender's lifetime, could be described as karma, but the guides simply don't support the idea that we carry karma with us from one existence to the next. If we go back to the analogy of the dramatic production, each life is like a different show: we all play characters, but when that production finishes its run, we move on to the next play. In other words, it would make no sense for Hamlet to walk into the middle of a production of *The Sound of Music* and be killed by German soldiers as payback because he brought about the demise of his malicious stepfather. When a life or production is complete, we don't undergo judgment and then experience the old "eye for an eye" retribution in another incarnation.

If it is true that we only experience some present-life internal strife for our bad deeds, then what is the incentive to be good? One of the most powerful motivations is that you are able to keep the positive aspects of your soul and build on those within each existence. That is your ascension. It is an upward trajectory that gets better and better as your consciousness grows. It is what is referred to as dharma, the positive energy and enlightenment you carry with you, and, unlike negativity, that positive growth *is* carried forward through the multiple layers of existence. Kelsey explains:

Kelsey: The flipside side of the coin is dharma which is the positives that we experience, the joy, the love. That doesn't fade. That actually stays and that too becomes a memory, so we come back into a new incarnation, if we had been a loving person before, full of love and compassion, that's going to resonate in this incarnation. You can't get rid of it.

Dharma stays with us, continually growing, and that is comprised of the positive elements of our spiritual being.

I asked Roxanne's guides, several angels and an ascended master, about the concept of karma.

JS: So what can they [your guides] tell us about this belief system [karma]?

Roxanne: It is a limited belief system that humans have created as a rationale for their lack of manifestation.

JS: What does that mean?

Roxanne: You create your own destiny. It is the path you choose and not retribution. It is the learning, [with emphasis] *learning*. When things are hard, you learn. It is easier for people to think it's their karma, but it's a part of their learning and growing.

JS: So karma is not about punishment?

Roxanne: No.

JS: It's really about us picking lessons to learn? Is that what karma is about in the spiritual world?

Roxanne: Yes.

JS: If there was karma with punishment, wouldn't that involve judgment?

Roxanne: There is no punishment.

JS: And is there judgment, on the other side?

Roxanne: No.

JS: So this concept doesn't really work except in humankind?

Roxanne: They said it is a weak-minded human thing. It's the 3-D thinking.

JS: What does that mean?

Roxanne: Limited human beliefs.

The guides often reference "3-D thinking" as a way of saying that humans sometimes don't embrace the multitude of dimensions that make up the Universe. That limited thinking could enable us to blame our lack of manifestation on karma. In other words, when we fall short of our goals or are unhappy with the way things have unfolded in our life, it is easy for humans to assume it was due to a sort of leveling out of energy based on what has occurred in past existences. Roxanne's guides disagree with that line of thinking and suggest that the real truth about karma may lie in what we are here to learn. Roxanne's guides unambiguously share this insight when they go on to say: "It is the path you choose and not retribution. It is the learning, learning."

Perhaps a better way of describing karma might be that it is the learning we have chosen to further our enlightenment. Cheryl's angels and spirit guide talk about lessons as opposed to punishment.

JS: If we do something wrong, if we hurt someone, is there such a thing as karma? How does that work?

Cheryl: Those kinds of things are just lessons, opportunities for people to heal deeper, to become more. Karma isn't created by wrongdoing. Karma is part of the experience.

JS: Karma is part of the lesson?

Cheryl: Yeah. Everybody has to experience these lessons in order to evolve and become that next level of being enlightened.

JS: So karma might be that if you do something wrong, you feel bad that you did it and then decide never to do that again?

Cheryl: If you do something that hurt somebody, it actually might be for that person's highest good, so it's really not about doing something wrong or bad. Sometimes when you do things like that, it actually creates an opening for another human to heal, as well as for you to learn that judgment is a negative energy. So once you learn how to not judge, your energies open.

Once again, the perspective about karma as a *learning* experience is being reinforced. The notion that if we hurt someone, that interaction might be "for that person's highest good," suggests that some of our actions might, on the surface, appear to be bad, but in the grander picture might actually promote personal growth. For example, if we commit a minor offense against someone, the objective behind that transgression might be for them to practice forgiveness and let go of their anger. It appears that, as we all navigate our spiritual journeys, the web of lessons connecting us can be extremely intricate. Bad things have to happen in the world for us to face the challenges that are going to facilitate our learning, so we all have to experience bad things and *do* some bad things as well. Without that, there would be no conflicts, and it is those conflicts that subsequently lead to insights. Instead of looking at those negative actions with "judgment," we need to instead ask how that situation might help us grow and evolve.

> JS: And when we make our transition, do we experience karma in the afterlife? In other words, if you do something wrong in this life, you're going to pay for it in the next life.
>
> Cheryl: No, not really. It's just evolvement. It's more like if you don't have the opportunity to really feel and learn lessons, you'll get another opportunity. It's not really karma; it's an opportunity to experience it again, so that it can be healed.

We have the "opportunity" in each lifetime to learn from our actions. We don't receive payback; instead, we get another opportunity in another existence to try to understand what we didn't fully grasp in this incarnation.

The traditional belief that karma can help us justify actions and events we can't understand, and it can reassure us that bad people will eventually pay for their malicious deeds, works well for our human minds. However, the guides—at least about 95 percent of them—don't agree with that dynamic. That is a human perspective and not the way it works from the grander perspective of the Universe.

Some guides did say that karma can manifest in our present lives in the form of inner turmoil. The misdeeds one commits might lead to guilt or fear or unhappiness within the life that that deed was committed. Although those who were wronged might feel like it evens the score a little, our learning will not take place if we sit back and hope for others to suffer internally, or eternally, for what they have done. Our growth comes in the form of forgiveness and release.

What it all seems to come down to is karma is really about new understandings that emerge from the life plan that we chose for ourselves. Hard lessons might seem like payback when, in actuality, they are designed to help us make greater leaps in our personal evolution. We grow by participating in the learning that comes through difficult situations. We regress if we try to attach blame or judgment, or resign ourselves to pass off our lessons as prior life settlements.

So, if we look back at that past life I described at the beginning of this chapter, was my adversary wanting to settle the score with me because I fired that pistol before the official reached the count of one? No, that would be using human logic and justification—and karmic rationalization—to try to explain a difficult current life situation. In that prior incarnation, it is more likely that I might have experienced an internal punishment: perhaps I felt guilt or cowardice for the remainder of that life. But in this life, I have to release that idea of karmic retribution. I am a different actor following a different script, and my perspective about that person needs to shift from payback to what I am supposed to learn from that relationship and what lies within that conflict that might enable me to grow.

# Chapter 7

# What Is the Nature of Illness and How Do We Heal?

As a healer, I have always been searching for that long-lost technique or secret healing method that would generate incredible curative breakthroughs. I would read about, study, experiment with, and observe various healing modalities whenever I could. I have always had some interest in modern innovations, but the true fascination for me came from learning about methods that may have faded with time, whether it was the ways of the mystical shamans or even the techniques used by the ancient Greeks and Egyptians.

Like most alternative healers, I have had many amazing success stories, and I am very grateful for that, but I have also observed a small percentage of the population that no one was able to help. These were the people who failed with both Western medicine as well as the complementary modalities. That is why I wanted to know more about the techniques and modalities that might have been lost through time. Maybe there was some hidden knowledge that could help those people who were slipping through the cracks. That set me on a quest to find the magic cure or forgotten procedure that would help everyone.

That pursuit has provided some interesting twists and turns. One of those intriguing moments occurred when I was invited to join a group of colleagues in a guided meditation that had each of us imagine we were going back in time to a healing center from the antiquities. The leader of the group was extremely careful not to describe any of the details of the center or what the healing processes were like. She was making sure she didn't lead us or put any visuals in our heads. The session was quite profound for me. After we were done, I was reluctant to reveal what I experienced because I thought what happened to me was going to be too extreme for anyone to believe. But when others started to share, I was stunned to hear that not only did they have the exact same experience, but the healing temple and many of the healing techniques were almost identical to what I had undergone.

I left that session asking myself how all of the participants in that group could have experienced the same thing, unless, I speculated, we truly had all been there before. Could it have been something we had all participated in, perhaps in a past life, and it had been buried in our subconscious memories? I wondered if this was what I was looking for: a long-forgotten process that we practiced centuries— or, more accurately, millenniums—ago when we had the knowledge of and performed healing techniques that were far more powerful than anything in our present consciousness. Was this something I could access and use with my clients? Would this work for those individuals struggling to heal?

So, I experimented with a process that took place within the ancient healing temple, using the mystical techniques that have been shared with me through time, working with Divine healers from multiple dimensions, and focusing on healing the energetic body.

That work seemed very profound, but I still found myself wanting to know more.

So, I kept searching and that led me to a woman who communicated with and channeled information from an archangel. A group of us gathered together to meet with her and each of us was allowed to ask for a channeled answer to one question. Most people asked questions like when they would find their life purpose or when they might meet their true life partner or when they might manifest prosperity. And then there was me. When it was my turn, I asked her about healing methods, from generations past or even from other realms, secrets that might unlock wellness for all.

She did share a few insights, but also pointed out that for some individuals, healing may not be part of their path. I understood that, but didn't want to accept it. I wondered if that notion could be reprogrammed with hypnotherapy, and I was still curious about secrets or methods that had either been lost or, perhaps, suppressed by generations of civilizations that had been fearful of unconventional healers.

To some extent, that dynamic, in which there are factions of our society that feel threatened by alternative healers, still exists today. There are numerous examples of that from the suppression of Rife technology to attacks on beneficial supplements coming from the FDA and the drug companies. For decades, the Western medical community has been trying to convince us that everything that happens within our bodies was strictly physiological and that our mind, emotions, and spirituality have nothing to do with what happens with our health and wellness.

A perfect example of this disconnect has been commonplace in the area of infertility. That is a field that has been a specialty of mine since I opened my practice, and I have documented my work in that area in a book called *The Mind-Body Fertility Connection* (Llewellyn, 2008). Many of my fertility clients were being told by doctors that their infertility was strictly physiological. Currently, in the United States, seven million women a year are being told that the roots of their infertility are solely physical and then given the diagnosis of "unexplained infertility." Essentially, they are being told the problem is physical, but their doctors can't find anything physically wrong that might be causing the infertility. That is an interesting contradiction, especially when it is happening seven million times a year.

Often, because these women have been told their problem was strictly physical, they were discouraged from or saw no reason to explore what was going on in their mind and emotions. But how could a realm that involves miscarriages, abortions, inappropriate sexual actions, sexual relationships, sexual abuse, sexual histories, dysfunctional relationships, low self-esteem, incredible vulnerability, religious dogma, and societal influence creating guilt about sexual behaviors *not* be in any way connected to the mind and emotions?

Yes, there has always been a medical mindset in which everything had to be scientifically verified, but there actually is a great deal of scientific evidence proving that there is connection between the mind and body when it comes to fertility, which I have documented in my book. And, yes, there has always been a Western medical business model that wants to ensure there is no competition, but at what point do those attitudes create a loss of credibility? And at what point does this violate the tenet of doing no harm? If a patient isn't given the tools to heal, is that ethical?

Fortunately, times have changed. Many have grown wiser. In our present world, more medical doctors are starting to disagree with that outdated view that the mind and emotions have nothing to do with our physical health. Patients are becoming more educated about their health and experiencing a multitude of benefits from alternative healing modalities.

What I have learned from working with fertility clients and about healing in general is that a key part of the process *is* about addressing the emotional roots. I have witnessed that when a cancer patient has a tumor removed and never does any emotional work around why the cancer developed inside them, the cancer often returns. Conversely, I have seen many cancer patients delve into the mental and emotional roots of their condition, and after completing the emotional healing, go into complete remission.

So, personally, I believe that we have to address the roots or the source of a disharmony as part of any treatment program if we want to create wellness. I'm not sure if there truly is a secret healing technique to use on those individuals who can't overcome their physical challenges or if there are people who are just not meant to heal. This is where I wanted more insight from the guides. What do they say about healing? How do we heal? What wisdom did they have to offer?

In one of the first *One Voice* sessions I conducted, I asked this question of Tim's guides, a totem and a diamond-shaped light. There was no hesitation in this blunt and succinct response.

JS: Why do disharmonies happen in our bodies?

Tim: Neglect.

JS: Neglect of what?

Tim: Of which we're here for, lessons.

In Chapter 4, the guides made it clear that we are here to learn lessons and ignoring those lessons can have an adverse affect on our health. This response was consistent with the earlier information and indicates that health issues happen for a reason and we need to be looking at *why* these disharmonies occur.

If we ignore our lessons, can we heal? I asked this question to Steven, who was working with a couple of spirit guides during his session.

JS: I have a question about healing. If someone has something physically wrong during this lifetime, can they heal?

Steven: Yes. I'm hearing that yes they can heal, but that doesn't mean the physical body will change.

When Steven says he is hearing, it means he is relaying the information he is being told by his guides. I was intrigued by the suggestion that one can heal, "but it doesn't mean the physical body will change."

JS: That implies that healing is not about the physical body. It's really about what?

Steven: The mental, emotional, spiritual journey and lessons.

Again, the focus is on our lessons. Our physical ailments are not just physical. The old medical model that insists our ailments are strictly physical may, in fact, be *preventing* people from healing because we have been conditioned to believe that it is okay for us to ignore the mental, emotional, and spiritual aspects of our afflictions.

We have been led to believe that healing is mending the physical body, but healing, as viewed by the guides, is much broader because it is about healing the spirit or soul. That is why the answer was yes, you can heal, but it doesn't mean the physical body will change. Healing means different things in this context; to humans, it is about the physical and to the guides it appears to be more spiritual.

JS: So people could heal, but the physical body may still keep its affliction.

Steven: Yes.

JS: If someone has something affecting them physically should they...

Steven [interrupting]: They should be trying to physically heal because that may be their path.

JS: Should the focus be on pharmaceuticals or Western medical procedures or healing the mental and emotional or a combination of all these?

Steven: It depends on what their path is. Some, their path is to know how to heal their physical body through pharmaceuticals. Some it's their path to know how to heal it through natural means. Some is to not heal the body, but to heal the mind. Some is to heal the spirit and not the body. Everybody's different. Depends on what their lesson is, what they're learning, what they need to heal. It might not be the body they need to heal; it might be the mind and the spirit. An ill body can help to heal the mind and spirit and vice versa.

This implies that the modality used for healing may be somewhat irrelevant compared to the evolution that is connected to the illness. The more important part of the journey is whether or not someone works on their lessons. Often, an illness can inspire the individual to do the work they might have been neglecting. Within this answer, there was also the implication that sometimes part of the journey is that we may "not heal the body," which is hard for us to understand. It is important to remember that from the perspective of the Universe—or the guides, angels, and energies representing the Universe in these dialogues—we have a multitude of lifetimes (as noted in Chapter 2), so an incurable illness in one of those existences, if it helps us with our evolution, might be worth the sacrifice of a single lifetime on this planet. There is also a strong likelihood that we may have agreed to experience that physical disharmony as part of our life plan (as discussed in Chapter 4) in order to further our growth.

The energetic guide working with Carla, elaborates on how healing is a way to get us to pay attention to the potential understandings we have agreed to experience as part of our life plan.

JS: What about illness? Where does illness or disharmonies in the body come from?

Carla: Learning. It's all learning because some people need a bigger nudge to ask questions to get on their learning path, and some people need to stop in their tracks and have something like their illness because they won't get the other signs or they won't ask questions. Some people live their whole lives asking one question or very simplistic things, but they won't continue to peel the onion back, and so disease comes in to make everyone stop and to look at it a different way.

An illness generally makes a person become more introspective. It makes them "ask questions" such as "Why is this happening to me?" According to Carla's guide, the function of an ailment is to make that dialogue take place. But if physical disharmonies and challenges are designed to get us to look at our issues, one has to question the use of medications that prevent us from doing exactly that. Antidepressants and antianxiety medications sometimes create scenarios where we *don't* look at our issues. This runs contrary to the edict that we are here to learn lessons by addressing our issues. Are we suppressing the impetus that we are supposed to be acknowledging? There are many conditions that call for medical intervention, but is our society becoming overmedicated because we have been continually told that we need to turn to prescription drugs to cure whatever ails us?

Time and time again, the guides repeated that the best healing method or the best way to prevent the development of physical disharmonies is working on our mental and emotional challenges. Carla's guide explains:

JS: So if we paid attention to the signs of the learning behind an illness and picked up on that, that illness may not have happened?

Carla: Yes. It's all tied to emotions and spirit. Every disease has an emotional component. Every disease has a vibrational element to it. So, within your family of origin you pick up that you're wrong, you're evil, you're bad, and you become very negative, and so you're putting all this negative energy out there, and you're controlling and you're super harsh. That particular emotional pattern may manifest itself as cancer because it's eating away at your soul. It is eating away at who you are, and unless you correct that emotional pattern, it's going to keep coming back. It's the pattern that you need to break. You don't need to go with lasers beating out the cancer because the cancer's going to constantly come back, because that emotional pattern has never left, and it's the emotional pattern that you need to pick up, need to see what brought you to that place, and that allows you to ask questions. And it's the disease that gets you to stop to do somewhat of an internal check-in, and then if you turn away from the internal check-in, that's when it becomes aggressive.

Carla's guide says that "every disease has an emotional component," and the emotional roots of an illness need to be addressed for healing to occur. The example in this excerpt demonstrates how a negative self-perception that began within one's "family of origin" can mutate into a physical disharmony. Simply removing the tumor does not cure the outcome—in this case the cancer—nor does radiation, chemotherapy, or other medical treatments unless the root cause is unearthed and processed. This message was repeated constantly by the guides. Again, this flies against the old Western medical edict that our physical disharmonies are strictly physiological and have nothing to do with the mind and emotions.

JS: It sounds like what you're saying is that to heal, it's about coming back to center and loving ourselves and looking at our issues. So, how does Western medicine fit into this?

Carla: It's a distraction. There is some way to kind of structure you through this, because this work is terrifying to people. "What, I have to look at my life? I have to look at decisions I've made. I have to look at who I really am. Oh no. I'm taking a pill. No, no, no. Probe me, prod me, do something else. I'm not doing that. That's way too hard." And so in some ways the Western world creates the chaos for those who don't take the journey.

Taking a pill or using pharmaceuticals has become a way for some of us to avoid looking at the underlying issues and addressing the things we have come here to learn. To clarify, the guides aren't saying we should all stop taking the drugs that are vital to maintaining our health and well-being; that could potentially be dangerous. Instead, they are advising us not to overlook the emotional roots of our disharmonies. Perhaps an antidepressant is necessary, but coupling that with some form of therapy to look inward at the source of the discomfort might be appropriate. And perhaps the bigger area of concern is the commercial advertisements that present a dynamic that suggests we can solve all of our problems by taking the right pill. In some cases, those drugs are absolutely necessary, but I believe the guides are cautioning some individuals not to utilize drugs to foster a state of denial or avoidance.

When it comes to mental and emotional challenges, feeling disconnected from spirit can create internal strife as well as physical disharmonies. Blake, working with Source, talks about how this happens.

> Blake: We look at everything as a physiological issue. But it's all spiritual. Those who are depressed, it is usually because they have forgotten that they are a spirit being having a human experience.

Our emotional struggles often have a spiritual component. Through the use of science, there has been an attempt to shift the emphasis from the emotional and spiritual to the physical by looking at things like brain chemistry. Once a condition can be diagnosed and classified as *physical*, then that can justify using a drug for treatment. Although that fits perfectly into the Western medical model, are we really helping people by taking them away from the underlying issues?

> Blake: You, yourself [referring to me, the author, whose work focuses on the relationship between the mind and body],

know the mind-body connection: what you believe is what your body is going to manifest. If you believe a pill is going to help you, it may, but you're not really fixing the problem, you're just dealing with the symptom. You might not feel as down, but you're not really going to connect. You have to feel that depression. That's your spirit's way of being in pain. When your body feels pain, especially severe pain consistently, you go to a doctor and they try to repair it. It's no different with depression. It's the soul's way of saying "I'm in pain because I'm not connected," and the only way to get over that is to connect. But if you don't believe there is such a thing as Source, and you don't believe there is anything when you die, how can you reconnect with that which you don't believe in, so you'll spend your life that way.

Perhaps one of the less acknowledged components of our physical and emotional disharmonies might be the lack of connection with the Divine. It isn't so much that people don't want to connect with spirit as much as that they never learned an appropriate way to do so. During the last several decades, a significant number of people have left their churches because they didn't resonate with the approach, the beliefs, or the dogma of traditional religions. The emphasis on genuine spirituality—one's personal connection with Divine energy—had become lost. That individualized approach often wasn't a part of organized religion. In a sense, people who didn't resonate with the large institutions became spiritually homeless because there was no place to learn how to create a personal relationship with the Divine. The guides, in many of these interviews, seem to be telling us that our disharmonies—including some emotional struggles—might be occurring because it is "the soul's way of saying I'm in pain because I'm not connected."

Fortunately, things have changed. There are new churches that encourage each individual's spiritual growth. There are books, courses, and speakers that can help enlighten without coercion. Unfortunately, many of those lost individuals have become disillusioned and are reluctant to explore spirituality again or are unsure how to begin that process, but it is that spiritual connection, according to Blake's guide, that might be crucial to our physical and emotional well-being.

With those people who are addressing their issues and are on a path of healing, I asked Courtney's guide, Archangel Raphael, what is the best way for that healing to occur.

JS: When there is illness or a physical disharmony in a human being and assuming that their path is to heal, how does one do that? We have everything from Western medicine and pharmaceuticals to alternative healing modalities. If our goal is to heal, and that is part of our path or journey, how do we go about that?

Courtney: You continue to look at the vibrations and be present to what is true. If there is something that is present that is based in fear and greed, it is not helping. If the truth is to heal human bodies, you must go with what supports the human body, and there should be no debate about there's only particular energies that support that body. You are given everything on this planet to heal, to sustain, to support, enabling the body to live fully.

In the course of these dialogues, more and more attention has turned to the fact that we are energy and our bodies are energy. So when I asked about how to heal—in those cases in which one is paying attention to their lessons and has a life plan where there is the potential to heal—the focus often turned to our energetic bodies. Naturally, there are healing modalities such as acupuncture and herbal medicines that work with the chi or energy in our bodies, but there is also what I refer to as our essence frequency.

I use that phrase, *essence frequency*, to describe the overall vibration or aura that emanates from each individual. For example, if someone approaches you and you get a sense that they are creepy or angry, you might pick up on that impression and be sure to stay out of their way. That is their essence. When people are fearful or greedy, that becomes their essence frequency.

Someone who is filled with inner peace has a different energy from someone who is consumed by greed. Our essence frequency is a reflection of who we are inside. It is a manifestation of our consciousness. In theory, we are trying, in each existence, to generate an essence energy that is in sync with Divine energy. As we evolve, our energy becomes lighter, brighter, and filled with love. Archangel Raphael is saying that healing can't take place within people who are filled with greed or fear. Our overall vibration changes as we do our inner work. In other words, as we evolve, our energy changes. The work we do on our issues is reflected in our consciousness, which, in turn, makes us emanate an essence frequency that is full of light and doesn't vibrate with many of the human disharmonies. In other words, an elevated consciousness is a way of being less susceptible to illness and, potentially, a means through which we can heal our ailments.

While on the topic of energetic frequencies, Courtney's guide addressed the business aspects of Western medicine and why there are some characteristics of that modality that fail to resonate at a healing vibration.

Courtney: If you are to look at the things that are utilized in what is called Western medicine, you must look at the truth of what drives that, what drives that force? There is no healing that would be withheld or controlled or not allowed to every person that would need it. That, by itself, says it's not healing, if it is not universally allowed to anyone who would need it. The intent behind such medicine does not vibrate at a level that would heal.

These comments might be a reference to the fact that some drugs, treatments, and procedures can be cost prohibitive or unavailable to large segments of our population. Although there are doctors who do pro bono work, much of Western medicine is profit-driven. Greed, as mentioned earlier, is not a vibration that resonates with Divine energy—or wellness—whether it is the energy of an individual or an industry as a whole.

JS: If healing is increasing our vibrational frequencies—and I might be oversimplifying this—it sounds like healing is about becoming more connected with the oneness, the love, the light, and letting go of the past and things we've been holding onto. In other words, maybe it is about raising our frequency, and it is not so much about the drug we're taking?

Courtney: Yes, you need to work with the vibrations of the entire planet. It all needs to elevate if your goal is to have health and well-being across all people on the planet. Everybody needs to work towards a common goal and not a selfish goal. Greed has no place if the world wants to elevate.

Courtney's guide emphasizes that healing could elevate to a much higher level if the energetic vibration of all people were to rise. Greedy or selfish individuals or industries pull the collective energy, and the collective health, of the planet down.

Any discussion about healing should include an acceptance that we live in bodies that are mortal. Our bodies, with time, are meant to wear out. We must keep in mind that illness is a way for us to make our transition out of the human physical body. Jackie's spirit guide mentions this in our dialogue.

JS: What is the nature of physical illness or disharmony in the body?

Jackie: Well, the physical body does wear out. It is a fallible vehicle to different diseases and the different things that come about for different souls.

Although our souls may be immortal, our physical bodies do need diseases and infirmities, from time to time, to move us on to other incarnations. We have to accept that "the physical body does wear out. It is a fallible vehicle...." Quite bluntly, when it is time to move on, we sometimes need physical issues to bring about death.

As I look back at my ideas about healing prior to these conversations with the guides, I was both right and wrong in some of my preconceived ideas and approaches. I was right in that the focus of my work has always been to explore the underlying source or causes of illness and then attempt to process those emotional roots. According to the guides, that is the most important part of healing because that involves the client addressing their issues, which means they are working on their lessons.

In my attempt to uncover the secret healing technique or magic bullet that was going to help the clients who weren't benefiting from Western medicine or alternative modalities, I discovered that the method used may not be as important as the individual's journey. People who are doing their personal work and have selected a life plan in which they can heal may find success in any one of a number of modalities. However, there are people who may not achieve wellness—regardless of the modality they choose—because of two considerations.

1.  Some individuals have agreed, through their life plan, not to heal. It is an agreement in which the healing may occur on a soul level, but the physical body might not recover. That person may have agreed to come into this incarnation with a covenant to pass away from a physical ailment. It might be that their learning takes place through the illness and transition. It is almost like a business contract where their life was set to come to completion from a predetermined cause. It appears that there is no healing process, Western or otherwise, that can change that.

2.  The other consideration is that it appears that working on our lessons is a part of creating wellness. Resisting or trying to avoid or deny our issues might be contributing to the dynamic that is making us ill. The guides suggested that, in some cases, if you don't work on your stuff, an illness might occur to push you into an introspective state. If you still resist, it appears that wellness may not be a possibility. An example of this is the cancer patient

who has a tumor removed and, for a short time, goes into remission. If the underlying emotional or spiritual cause of the disharmony is not addressed, it is possible that a relapse will occur. Even the most advanced healing methods may not be enough to overcome the resistance to face our lessons.

For those who do address their lessons and are destined to heal, it appears that the actual modality itself may not be as important as their personal belief in that modality. In other words, if you believe that acupuncture will heal you, then it will. If you believe energy work will heal you, it will.

Once again, this is all about our lessons. I know this sounds repetitive, but it came up with the guides in almost 100 percent of all the conversation about health. As a society, we sometimes overlook this, and that is probably why the guides bombarded us with this message. Many individuals refuse to work on their issues, whereas others will seek out a modality in which they can be healed without truly looking at their stuff. In recent years, there have been some new psychotherapeutic techniques introduced that claim clients can let go of issues without truly addressing those issues. Common sense tells us that this may not be realistic. Lessons can't be learned unless we truly address them, and, again, how can a client *learn* anything when the process they are using is designed to ensure they *avoid* looking at their stuff?

Other people claim that they "handle" their issues by handing their challenges over to God. Although the act of letting go is beneficial, if this is done in the spirit of denial, then trying to disown an issue by simply giving it away may not, in reality, be a means of healing. Thus, the lesson goes unlearned.

Those who have done their work often reflect an aura or essence energy of inner peace and unconditional love. Many people claim that they have done their work, but it is clear from the way they lead their lives and the aura they present whether they have been successful or not. Individuals filled with energies such as fear, greed, anger, denial, envy, selfishness, low self-esteem, or a sense of superiority still have work to do.

The guides also mentioned that spiritual alienation can sometimes be a factor in both physical and emotional issues. Depression was sometimes associated with individuals who felt disconnected from having a spiritual path. The implication was that establishing a greater sense of oneness can sometimes boost our moods.

So, how do we apply this guidance to circumstances where illnesses seem completely illogical or defy our human, rational, understanding? What about, for example, those heart-breaking situations such as when a young child comes onto this planet, becomes stricken with cancer, and dies at age 6? In those cases, it helps to look at the larger picture of how people can grow and evolve from the situation. I asked Jackie, working with Archangel Raphael, about these types of situations, and here was the response:

> Jackie: It could be that this is the soul's way of choosing its demise of its physical body, and that is also useful to the soul in helping others that love that person to grow and to experience the pain that helps some go to higher and more expansive levels to find that connection with the Divine or to reconnect.

What does this response mean and how can we apply it to a real life situation such as that 6-year-old who dies of cancer?

Suppose many of the people sharing the same soul group as the 6-year-old—such as their friends and birth family—needed to learn compassion and empathy because, as a group, they had been self-centered and lacked compassion. That soul with cancer chooses to help the group advance by agreeing to the illness. Everyone in the group is devastated by the "tragedy" and the "loss," but they all come out of that experience changed. They learn how to be caring, empathetic, and supportive.

What about the 6-year-old? What would be the lesson for him or her? Perhaps that individual had never been able to feel or accept love and being the recipient of unconditional love was the goal of that lifetime. The illness creates an outpouring of love from family and friends. The 6-year-old accepts it and for all subsequent existences has enabled themselves to give and receive unconditional love. From the perspective of the humans involved, the whole ordeal is an upsetting tragedy. From the Universal perspective, that existence was a huge victory because the love and compassion learned by the entire group can now continue to grow and multiply, elevating the consciousness of the planet. The soul who incarnated as the 6-year-old willingly agreed to take on that role because of the immense benefits to the entire soul group. And remember: if we have thousands of existences, that one lifetime might be one small speck on the continuum of our existence.

Finally, with regards to Western medicine, the guides were opposed to cases in which an individual was using allopathic medicine to avoid addressing their issues. The communications were not saying that we shouldn't take prescriptions, because there are situations where drugs are necessary. Instead, I believe the message was not to overlook or disregard the source or roots of the issues that challenge us, because that is how we uncover and process the lessons that help us evolve. In other words, consider some form of therapy or deeper work as part of whatever healing path you choose.

Another issue the guides had with Western medicine occurs when the intention behind it is about profit and control. Naturally, there are always exceptions to this. Some members of the Western medical establishment embrace healing the mind, body, and spirit, whereas others want us to believe that they are the only ones who know how to heal and alternative modalities are ineffective and not a good investment. The guides argued against the latter and said it isn't so much about the modality chosen as long as the lessons are addressed and that healing is part of the life plan.

Are there ancient healing methods that can assist in healing? The verdict may still be out on that one. What I have discovered is that when an individual works with mind-body healing, it gives them an incredible sense of empowerment. Instead of waiting for the next treatment or procedure, they can actively feel like they are contributing to their well-being by incorporating mind-body healing into their self-hypnosis. How effective is that? We don't know for sure. We have yet to fully discover how powerful the mind—especially in deeper states of consciousness—can be.

## Chapter 8

# Why Are Humans on This Planet?

A few years ago, in our travels, my wife and I found ourselves flying over the Andes Mountains to an isolated village by the name of Coca. In Coca, we got on board a slow motorized boat and rode for two and a half hours down the Napo River, one of the tributaries that flow into the Amazon. At the end of that boat ride, we pulled up to what appeared to be a fairly inconspicuous dock, where we disembarked and hiked for a half mile through the steamy jungle. Most of the walk was on raised bamboo walkways because the flooding rains would cause the tributaries to swell, washing out any trails that weren't elevated off the ground. At the end of the trek, we came upon a secluded area where three dugout canoes were waiting for us. Our guides rowed the canoes for another mile, along a slow, moving river and then across a vast freshwater lake. With each leg of the trip, we moved deeper into the rain forest, where the vegetation became more wild and lush. From those canoes, as the sun was setting, we saw night hawks, tiger egrets, herons, and flycatchers.

That night, after we arrived at our camp, our guide offered to take us back out on the lake in one of the canoes. There was so much to see in the jungle after dark and he wanted to share that with us. Our guide had learned to identify more than a thousand types of birds by their call or their songs; he lived in harmony with the Earth and knew the sounds of the rainforest because he'd grown up observing, watching, and listening to the wildlife.

There was no moonlight when we paddled out on the lake that night. The water was completely still. There were no lights or life jackets, and we were many, many miles from civilization. There were bats flitting about above us in the night sky. There was a tree boa dangling from a branch waiting for an unwitting prey. Using flashlights we were able to scan the shoreline, where we could see the eyes of the caimans waiting by the water's edge. Our guide told us stories about the paiche, a giant fish that lived in the lake and was powerful enough to turn over any boat or canoe that wandered into its territory. The stories weren't myths, they were true, and on one of our expeditions out on the lake, the paiche came to the surface and rammed our boat. But we weren't scared. We were awestruck by the beauty and how everything fell perfectly into place.

Finally, after our journey, when it came time to rest, we slept in straw huts with thatched roofs and uneven floors. The huts were built on stilts to protect them from rising waters during the rainy season. There was no electricity after dark. The beds were checked for insects and then we surrounded ourselves with mosquito netting to sleep. Once we settled in, the sounds of the night—the owls, the frogs, the night birds, the monkeys, the animals, and the insects—came alive. There was something about that sound that was incredibly calming to the limbic brain. And then when the whisper of a comforting, soft, cool rain began, it felt like I belonged: I felt a profound connection to the Earth.

It is difficult to capture in words the essence of a pristine rainforest. Everything is alive. You can almost feel the Earth living and breathing. The vitality of plants, the birds, the animals, and the insects make it seem as if the rainforest is an entity in itself. But at the same time there is a stillness in the surroundings that generates an incredible sense of inner peace. The verdant beauty and the vibrant energy of the jungle, bursting with life, helped us remember that essential connection we have with our planet: it gives us everything we need to sustain life.

This was how the Earth used to be. This was our world. This is what the Earth was like centuries ago when everything was wild. This is what it was like before man came in and took much of the life away. There are still places you can find that energy. A walk through the redwoods can touch something deep in the soul that most of us have forgotten.

God or Spirit or the Divine energy created what by all appearances might be the most amazing planet in the galaxy, perhaps in the universe. Nature had a balance between the plants and animals that was perfectly orchestrated. Then man arrived and created an industrialized world that interrupted that equilibrium.

What if man had never been created and the planet was free of pollution and global warming? What if all the extinct and endangered animals still roamed the Earth? What if that majestic energy that still lives deep in the rainforest was present throughout the land? That was the next set of questions for the guides. Why are we here? Why does this world need us? Is there hope for us, or are we on a course to destroy the planet and ourselves in the process?

I started these conversations by questioning why we are here. In this case, I was not asking why we are here as individuals. I was asking why humankind inhabits this planet. When I broached the topic of why humans exist, I expected some deep philosophical answers that might be hard to comprehend. Instead, the initial answer seemed very logical and tapped directly into one of the concepts from Chapter 1. It related to the notion that we—our souls or spirits or consciousness—are all energy. Nora, who was working with her guardian angel, helped shed light on this subject.

JS: So why does God need us? God created this beautiful planet with animals and plants and trees and birds, so why did God create humans?

Nora: To give us a little taste of what it's like to live as a human versus pure energy. To touch, feel, taste, love, connect, be flesh.

The answer made perfect sense. If we are energy, how can we truly experience life? We need physical form to learn and grow in a tangible way. How could we "touch, feel, taste, love" and connect with other humans if we are simply energy? We had to take on a solid form and experience emotions in order to feel love and participate in life's dynamics, and it is those dynamics that allow us to have the opportunity to learn lessons so we can evolve.

One way to look at this would be to imagine our conscious energy as vaporous steam that is simply floating around in the atmosphere. If that steam was transformed into ice or water, it might be able to sense temperature changes when it became hot or cold, but that steam would need to become part of the 65 percent of water that makes up a physical body in order to feel emotions and take part in the life dynamics that can assist in life's lessons. We needed to become flesh in order to participate in life; otherwise, we are energy and it is much more difficult to make tangible connections. Thus, one of the reasons for our physical existence is to have physical experiences that might otherwise be impossible if we consistently stayed in a state of pure consciousness.

Sylvia, working with Archangel Raphael, echoed that same perspective but added that, by becoming physical beings, we are also able to experience Divine energy in a palpable way. It should be noted that in these discussions, there are different descriptors for Divine energy. With Nora, in the first excerpt of this chapter, the word *God* was used because it had been employed earlier in our dialogue with her guardian angel, so I continued to use that same word to maintain consistency. In the exchange with Sylvia's archangel, the Divine had been described as "the Oneness" in answer to an earlier question, so I used that same expression for clarity.

JS: We look at this planet which is a beautiful place with the oceans, the mountains, the deserts, the animals, the birds. And then there's man. Why does the Oneness create man? By all appearances, it looks like we're messing a lot of things up on this planet.

Sylvia: Oneness experiences everything at all moments. It wants to experience all vibrations and is experiencing all vibrations. It came to many places in many forms, and it allowed free will to choose and then experience new things given those choices.

JS: So the Oneness is like an energy. If it wants to actually feel or experience, part of that is becoming three-dimensional?

Sylvia: Yes, or fifth-dimensional or seventh-dimensional and on and on.

This answer confirmed the idea that energy, whether it is Divine energy or our spirit energy, which we share with Divine, does need a solid form in order to learn, participate, feel, evolve, and experience. It is through us, when we become human, that Divine energy has a means to experience and create. This is happening on multiple levels. We, as humans, are able to feel and create, but on another level, the Divine is feeling, creating, and manifesting through us. We often think in terms of our world being three-dimensional, but, often in these discussions, we are quickly reminded that there are many more dimensions than we can comprehend. Being co-creators with the Divine is far beyond a three-dimensional phenomenon.

Margaret's two guides, an essence of color and a spirit guide who resembled a Greek philosopher, elaborate on the discussions about the vast multitude of dimensions that exist in the Universe and how our human manifestation might be a means to obtain knowledge and undergo palpable experiences for both us and for the Divine. In these conversations, the descriptor used for the Divine was Source.

Margaret: The source of all creation is the source of all the higher selves, and there are an innumerable number of higher selves in different dimensions in different physical embodiments. Some may be pure energy. Some may be embodied into a physical body, solid, something that you would understand as physical. There is a greater, a great Source, what we would call the Source of the Universe that has extended its arms and its experiences and its end points are the higher selves of us. If I am looking out at this Source, it is a point in the void with multitudes of flows of energy ending in points which then have multitudes of flows of energy, ending in points that are experiences. The purpose of these—I have a sense of it, but even I can't say its ultimate purpose—but the sense is that there is a desire of knowledge, there is a desire of experience, there is a curiosity, and there is love emanating from the Source and there is something that's more like curiosity and happiness as a child. It's very much like a child, with its fingers outstretched in touching every possibility in order to experience it.

The end points or "higher selves" take on human form in order to experience and gain knowledge not only for ourselves, but as a means for Source to manifest and discover through us. This situation is described much like a child that is reaching out to touch "every possibility in order to experience it." Source isn't directing us or telling us what to do; that would violate our prerogative of having free will. Instead, Source is energetically able to passively feel and experience through us.

In a sense, this passage captures a childlike wonder or innocence to this process. The comparison to a child is interesting because it implies that we begin our lives in a naïve, uncorrupted state. The question this raises is if that dynamic is something we are supposed to uphold and an indication of how we are supposed to live out our lives. Has the human race, instead, created so much negative programming—bombarding us from infancy—that we have forgotten our original childlike essence? Do we forget our innate state of love and compassion as we become enmeshed, through words and actions, in the darker aspects of humanity? Those questions are important because as these dialogues continued, the conversation turned more to what is the responsibility that comes with physical embodiment.

One of our main objectives in our physical existence, as expressed in earlier chapters, is to evolve to a higher vibration. "Free will," came up as an important factor in shaping that evolution, and the ability to choose opens up both positive and negative outcomes as it is a vital component in learning lessons. Addison's Native American shaman answers questions about free will.

JS: Why is that [free will] important?

Addison: So we can learn and we can understand all of the elements of creativity. This is not just Source that is doing this, or that that expression happens in an external way. It is that we are creation, and we can express that creation and not be separated from Source.

In Chapter 1, when the guides were asked about the nature of the Divine, we were told that there is no separation between humans and Source. We are Divine energy and we—humans—are part of the creation process. The Divine gives us the ability to create, but does not control what or how we create. That is where free will comes into play. In a sense, we are given the tools and sophistication to build what we choose. Divine energy gives us that capability and through each of us, Divine energy is able to feel and experience everything about each and every endeavor. But there is no interference: we are never told what to create.

JS: Are you saying that this is how we can recognize the source energy inside of us: because we are co-creators?

Addison: Just one second [as he listens for an answer]. It's deeper than that because it's not just recognizing that, it's *being* that creation, and in that there is also the responsibility that comes along with that. Do we understand *how* to do creation, *how* to participate in creation, how to be creation *in balance* so that we can fully express ourselves and have that in connection with Source so that we *don't* make a difference.

Many of us have been told that we are co-creators in our lives, but rarely does anyone mention the responsibility of being a co-creator. Are we creating in a way that is in "connection with Source"? I understood this to mean that we should look at what we create as an extension of the Divine. Are our actions and the world we create one of higher consciousness or are we doing things that can be exploitive or harmful to others. The last phrase about *not* making a difference is questioning whether or not we are creating in a manner that is *not* harming or taking. It is much like what hikers are told when they go into the wilderness: "leave only footprints." Footprints indicate that you did no harm. Is the world a better place from your influence or did you make a difference by taking, hurting, abusing, and using the world or the people around you? That is what is meant by responsibility and not making a difference by using the creation process strictly for personal gain.

When I asked Kendra's group of four guides about why we are here, the word *discovery* was used. As co-creators, the process of discovery gives us the opportunity to evolve: we can make negative decisions or follow a path based on more honorable actions.

JS: We have this beautiful, amazing planet with mountains and oceans and waterfalls and animals. Why put humans here? We warmed up the planet, we've polluted; some of the animals are extinct.

Kendra: This is a place of discovery and there is an energy to be evolved, so it's a part of our evolution. It has to do with the quality of energies, so even though there are the so-called negative places that have been developed on this planet, there is also this opportunity to bring forward more Divine and noble qualities They are heavier and more weighted than the parts that you bring up like that we're being disrespectful to the Earth. When a human being turns toward a more noble quality, that is the reason humanity's on Earth.

JS: Noble?

Kendra: A noble, greater, rising above.

The phrase "bring forward more Divine and noble qualities," again, suggests that humans have choices with regards to the footprint they leave on humanity. Even though free will implies it is okay to do whatever you want, each individual can choose to create in an honorable or noble fashion, or they can act in a way that merely supports their personal interests. It is easy to choose a life path that simply promotes the self-interest of the person on that journey, but it's the noble actions and the noble intentions that move people to higher levels of evolution and, subsequently, benefit the planet.

It is important to remember that just as each individual is comprised of a conscious energy field, humanity is comprised of our collective energy field. We are all a part of that aggregate mass of energy we refer to as society. Everything we think, do, and say contributes to the collective. Our purpose here is not just personal evolution; we are here to raise the consciousness of humanity. Kendra's guides expressed concern about the planet, but believe humanity will eventually embrace a higher state of awareness.

JS: We look at the world with wars and terrorism and pollution, is there hope for us?

Kendra: It is a very delicate balance right now, a very delicate balance. It could go either way.

JS: And what happens if we destroy our planet? What happens then?

Kendra: There's a grief, a sorrow that will be a sound that resonates through all areas if humanity doesn't turn towards a higher, more noble path, and we think they will. We think they will.

JS: Is there a way to help that along? For people who read this or get this information, what can they do? How can they make a difference?

Kendra: They can draw away from modern life that cultivates a sense of need. So if they can find within themselves a place that is not needing or wanting or grasping to get something more, so that they can turn within and find a quieting.

What can we do to generate a positive outcome? We should not approach life from a place of "needing or wanting or grasping to get something more." If our approach is self-centered and focused on what is in it for me, that consciousness is not in line with the higher good of that individual or the planet. The second part of that answer advises us to "turn within and find a quieting." That quiet, meditative or prayerful state is where we can find guidance about how to create from a place of responsibility.

Of all the topics discussed during these sessions, the one about the future of man and our existence on Earth was the one that generated the most disagreement. With most of the topics and questions broached in this book, the responses were amazingly consistent. But with this question, of whether the Earth can survive if we don't change our present course of action, the answers were more divided. Almost always, the preface to this one answer was essentially "We don't know." That was never the case with the other topics. With all the other replies—even the ones that humans seem most uncertain about, such as what happens when we die—there was never a moment of hesitation or even a hint of uncertainty, but when it came to what happens to our planet in the future, the answers were sometimes contrary and often indeterminate.

Some of the responses were more hopeful. Kathryn's radiant female guide foretells that the Earth will survive, but it will be changed.

JS: Is the Earth going to survive as we know it or does it change in some way?

Kathryn: Yes. It changes, but it is still the Earth. It is still the mother. The Earth will always be the Earth, but just as your bodies are holding more light, vibrating at higher frequencies, so will the Earth.

JS: Why do we need to become people and have a human experience? Couldn't Source energy have just created a perfect world without man? Why do we need the human experience?

Kathryn: So you can awaken to your joy. It's the Creator experiencing the Creator, which is you: the Creator experiencing itself.

JS: So, the Creator is energy, and it is wondering what it's like to be a human? I need to feel what my energy is like in a human.

Kathryn: Yes. Yes, and what is it like to awaken and know that you are the Creator.

JS: So we're all extension of the Creator?

Kathryn: Yes. Of course.

The spirit guide reinforces the perspective that we are the Creator and a part of the creation process. That is what is meant by these words: "It's the Creator experiencing the Creator, which is you: the Creator experiencing itself." There is an energy field for each individual, an energy field for humanity, *and* an energy field for the Divine. Each of us is a part of *all* of those fields. None of us is separate from the Divine. Part of our evolution is to undergo an awareness where each of us is to "awaken and know that you are the Creator." If each of us came to that understanding and to an acceptance of that responsibility, it opens the possibility of not only shifting the negative energies, but also the opportunity to manifest beautiful things. Imagine the dramatic changes that could occur if every action of each individual was directed from a place that consistently reflected unconditional love and light. If we each embraced the fact that we are a partner with the Divine and if everything we did reflected Divine love, the world would be a very different place. Instead, much of the old religious dogma insists that we are *separate* from the Divine. If this one aspect changed and each person operated from a place that honored Divine intention, then our approach to life would shift and, consequently, the humanity we have collectively created would be very different.

Although each individual's thoughts, beliefs, and actions can have a great deal of influence on what manifests in their personal life, the power of group thoughts can be incredibly powerful in shaping the energy of the planet. When we talk about what large groups of people believe, we are describing what is commonly referred to as the collective consciousness. We've all heard the adage that prayer is far more powerful when people gather in groups and pray together. That same principle applies to general attitudes, beliefs, fears, and judgments that are widely shared in society. What mainstream society believes creates an energetic power that can take on physical shape and cultivate tangible outcomes. An example of this occurred during World War II when people of Japanese ancestry were put into internment camps. The collective consciousness of the people in the United States at the time was one of fear, suspicion, and anger. Many feared that individuals of Japanese ancestry might be spies and our country could only be secure if those individuals were incarcerated. Others, perhaps feeling anger because of the attack on Pearl Harbor in 1941, may have felt the imprisonment was justified retribution. As a result, many innocent people were falsely interned and lost everything. That is merely one of many examples of how our collective consciousness has led to concrete consequences. Throughout history, prejudicial judgments about differences in race or religion have fueled countless battles. Those are negative examples of how group thought can lead to damaging outcomes.

Conversely, positive energy can have the opposite effect and generate positive results. The guides appreciate the power of the collective consciousness and are urging us to approach everything from a place of mindfulness so we can change the negative energies that have been so pervasive on our planet.

Our actions, thoughts, and intentions have power, and we can use that power to positively shape the world in which we live. When our mindset radiates "noble" qualities and is in alignment with the Divine, we can manifest a world of love and peace. When our intentions are not so pure, our world can become a place of greed, jealousy, anger, hostility, and fear. The manner in which our collective consciousness affects the world around us came up in a dialogue with Diane who was working with a master guide. The master guide would respond to questions by showing Diane visions of each answer. I asked the master guide how someone like Diane can personally influence what is happening in the world when, in most instances, we have no actual direct contact with the individuals who are responsible for those negative actions.

JS: If we aren't around those people who are responsible for negative actions; for example, if Diane can't talk to the leader of a terrorist group, what can she do? How does she change consciousness of this planet?

Diane: I don't really understand this, but he keeps showing me kids. I don't know what kids have to do with it. Group efforts, all working together.

Again, the guide is taking Diane to observe different scenes and giving her the opportunity to interpret what those visions mean. At first, she was unsure about the meaning attached to what she was seeing, a vision of kids coming together.

Diane: I guess it's prayer because he, again, is making the ripple effect, so we have to all work together with prayer. It doesn't matter what kind [of prayer], as long as we have that same energy working together. He's showing me knowledge again. Maybe it's getting knowledge out to the masses. Maybe the kids are like the new generation, and that's more important than what's already happening. But to get to the people who were already bringing harm to this world, I keep getting knowledge and group efforts, everyone working together.

Working together with prayer, regardless of what kind of prayer, opens up the possibility to generate change. I think the reason there is a clarification about "it doesn't matter what kind" is because prayer can take on many different forms. It can be traditional prayer, but prayer can be meditation or even a simple visualization process in which love and light are radiated out to the world. Perhaps kids appear in this visualization because the younger generations might be more open to new strategies of shifting our consciousness than those who have become more set in their ways.

JS: You mentioned prayer. Typically, we send negative energy to these people [for example, terrorists], but when you say "prayer," are you saying to send them positive energy?

Diane: Send them positive. I picture people standing in a circle holding hands. They must be praying, and they're not mad... I'm picturing the people in Whoville. They're all happy. So they're sending good energy and they're all holding hands, so it's a group effort.

The reference to Whoville comes from Theodor "Dr. Seuss" Geisel's popular children's book *How the Grinch Stole Christmas*. In that story, after the Grinch has stolen everything related to the celebration of Christmas, including all of the presents, from the residents of Whoville, the people gather together, join hands, and they sing and rejoice. Even though Seuss's message may have been to point out the real meaning of Christmas, it still serves as a good example to illustrate this argument. The act of people joining together with positive intentions created a shift in consciousness. When the Grinch hears the beautiful music and experiences the joy they collectively project, it changes him. His heart grows larger, he brings back all of the stolen goods, and he joins the people in their celebration. An outpouring of love, in that story, had the power to create positive change.

JS: They [the people of Whoville] send out love and light and look what happens. So what he [your guide] is saying is maybe that should be *our* strategy.

Diane: Yeah, yeah.

JS: Which is the opposite of what we've been doing.

Diane: Um-hm.

A simple children's story might be the perfect way to illustrate the power of our collective consciousness. We have become fixated on the idea that there is darkness or evil in the world. In many ways, we seem to surrender to that darkness and give it power and adopt the stance that nothing can be done to change it. The principle of the law of attraction is that our thoughts, beliefs, and emotions create our personal dynamics. It is also important to remember that the same process is used to make up the energy that forms our larger world and collective consciousness. If we participate in the communal anger, fear, and hatred every time there is a negative act in the world, we enable that harmful energy to grow and give it power. Each time we witness an act of terrorism in the news, we should look closely at how we respond. If we are overcome with fear and anger, then we are putting those negative thoughts and emotions into the collective consciousness and making that mass of damaging energy more formidable.

Conversely, if we are able to turn off those thoughts and consistently radiate love and forgiveness into the ether, it depletes the power from the negative factions. If we created an unwavering consciousness comprised of love, light, peace, and harmony—as the guides are telling us—then the world would be a very different place.

I asked Corrine's group of guides, including Archangel Uriel, how we should approach the negativity of the world today, and the answer was much like Diane's, a stark contrast to how most people currently respond to hurtful actions and caustic energies on the planet.

JS: How should we respond to things that are happening in the
world where people are making decisions that hurt others,
such as terrorists? Is there a way we can positively change
that dynamic?

Corrine: Send them love and forgiveness. That's all they [her
guides] just keep saying, is send them love and forgiveness.

This advice seems to contradict how most of the population consciously or subconsciously handles these situations at the present
time. We regard perpetrators with anger, hatred, fear, and con-
tempt. We certainly don't "send them love and forgiveness."

JS: Even the terrorists? Send them love and forgiveness.

Corrine: And healing energy.

JS: And if a lot of people did that and they received that energy,
might that create a shift in them?

Corrine: Yes, yes.

We can't be in charge of the behavior of others. We aren't responsible for anyone's path but our own, but the energy field that surrounds all of us can be changed. The choices an individual makes
might be different if they felt surrounded by love, rather than being
bombarded with anger and hatred.

Corrine: What they showed me before is that people will have
higher consciousness. They showed me across the world
[people] joining hands, but it's not hands, it's more like
energies, and sending forgiveness and healing energy, and
they showed me a push back. What they show me is more
like Asia and Saudi Arabia, they're pushing back. All that
green loving energy goes to them and they're pushing back.
They're pushing back. It's going to be very strong and
overwhelming for them, and they're going to push back.

JS: When you say push back, what does that mean?

Corrine: Surrender.

JS: They are going to surrender to that energy?

Corrine: Yeah, and they don't understand. They just stop. They just stop.

JS: So when we watch the 5 o'clock news and we get all angry and upset about these events, we are doing exactly the *wrong* thing?

Corrine: We are giving them power. [Long pause.] So they [her guides] are making that emphasis on groups. The power of group intention from many different ethnicities just uniting as one energy. That's what they show me.

JS: So if we can get together and send light and love and healing to these people in big groups, that has more potential to change things than what we're doing now.

Corrine: Yes.


If we look at this dynamic in terms of a Universal law of attraction, it appears that we are currently feeding the negative energy. If someone receives feelings of anger and hatred, they can only express behavior that reflects those attributes. If the terrorists were sent profound feelings of love and light, would it change their actions? That is what the guides are telling us.

If we look at this situation at a simplistic level, we could imagine a child who has been poorly treated by his or her parents. The parents yell, they hit, they belittle, they criticize, and they abuse. How could that child respond with anything but anger? How could that child know how to express love if they never felt it?

I'm certainly not defending the terrorists, nor am I rebuking our society for mishandling the way we have been responding to these situations. We are reacting as humans would with normal human emotions, but if this wisdom is right, we're doing everything wrong. Are we inadvertently, through the law of attraction, creating factions of society that are continually surrounded by feelings of hatred, anger, and malevolence?

I'm also not so idealistic to believe that this would immediately solve all of the world's problems, but what if it could create a shift? What if everyone on the planet sent love and light, on a consistent basis, to every soul on the planet? Could we change the collective consciousness? Could we use that same principle to create a planet that is glowing because it is encircled in a brilliant light emitted from billions of beings who are determined to create a new consciousness? (For those who are interested in bringing more light to the world, I've included a prayerful meditation at the end of this chapter that provides guidance for how to do that.)

Some people have been taught that the negativity in the world has such deep roots that it could never be eradicated. They have learned, especially through their religious upbringing, that there is truly a force of evil such as a devil or Satan or some sort of demon that is far more powerful than anything we can control with positive intentions. I asked Dina's spirit guide about this.

JS: One of the other concepts of man is that there is a devil or Satan.

Dina: [Laughs.]

JS: Why are you laughing?

Dina: Evil is in man. The gods are of love.

JS: So there is no Satan or devil?

Dina: No.

I wanted to clarify the semantics with this question. The implication with the word *evil* is that it is something beyond our control and perhaps even has an energy in itself. It brings up a feeling of helplessness and the possibility of a power that may never be defeated. "Negativity" is more of a description of someone who has strayed from their path. My questions were designed to determine if something existed that is truly beyond our control, or if we should instead be labeling incidents where people have stayed from their path as negative. I asked Dina's spirit guide if "negativity" is a better word for us to use in this context.

JS: So when we talk about evil, perhaps negativity is a better word.

Dina: It is. It's when you choose not to make things good when you're unhappy.

JS: So, it is more about negativity. It is not like people are possessed with evil?

Dina: No.

JS: That's a man-made description?

Dina: Yes.

The idea that there is no devil or Satan goes against much of what those of us who were exposed to traditional religious backgrounds have been taught. One client even shared with me the fear he had when he was growing up: he was afraid that if he ever left his church the devil would somehow "get him." That fear lasted into his 20s. He experienced a huge relief when his mindset changed and he no longer believed in the devil. The potential damage this generates occurs on both a personal and group level. It torments the individual as they live their life in fear. On the collective level, factions who believe in an evil power release a sense of fear and helplessness into the cosmos, as if some evil entity could potentially move in and take control at any time.

With each topic in these discussions, including this one about the possible existence of the devil, I would ask several clients the same question and then use a couple of passages that best represented the consensus among the guides. Samantha's archangel was in alignment with all of the other replies.

JS: Is there such a thing as evil? Is there a devil or Satan?

Samantha: No.

JS: I don't mean negative energy. I mean is there truly evil?

Samantha: No, no, no. No, there is no devil or Satan.

JS: Is it simply people who have gone astray...

Samantha [interrupting and continuing my thought]: who made that choice.

JS: So we don't have to worry about the existence of a devil who is going to try to come in and take our souls?

Samantha: No, it is your choice to be light or gray. So they [her guides] say coexisting contributes to the growth process for each, white and gray. Everyone started out with white, and with free will you choose to remain light or become gray or dark energy. They're your choices and contracts.

These comments are interesting in light of a discussion that occurred earlier in the chapter when a guide said that we come in with childlike innocence. In this instance, that innocence is described as coming in or being born as light and, through free will, we can "remain light or become gray or dark energy."

JS: So it [negativity] is really people just losing touch with that light and doing things that are more negative?

Samantha: Yes.

JS: Why was this whole idea of a devil created?

Samantha: They say that is a three-dimensional belief created by man because man is concrete and cannot understand that things exist as energy, and they need to put human form on every concept in order for it to fit into the three-dimensional realm.

Man created the devil concept because we needed to give negative energy a "form" or three-dimensional representation.

Samantha: It is negative thought forms and negative energy that they had to put into human form. They gave that power by doing that.

Again, I typically include only a couple passages that address each issue, I always try to pick the two or three that best represent the consensus of the responses. There were *no* guides who supported the idea that there is a devil or Satan or evil force that lurks in the shadows. For those who believe there is such a thing as an evil entity, it produces a great deal of internal fear. It generates a belief system that there is an evil power that is and will always be there. The belief in the existence of an unconquerable evil makes it very difficult to create a beautiful collective consciousness and visualize a world filled with love and peace.

Centuries ago, the concept of the devil was used to control parishioners by making them too fearful to ever leave the church or step outside the guidelines established by society. Spirituality, in contrast to that instilled dynamic, is about choosing for oneself what innately feels right. It is following internal guidance. It is okay for each of us to look at our inherited beliefs and decide which ones serve us and which ones don't. For some, letting go of the concept of the devil might feel liberating as the fear associated with those beliefs can be paralyzing.

In conclusion, what initially seemed like an easy question about our existence on this planet quickly became more and more complex. First, the human race is on this planet in order for us to feel and experience in a tangible way what would not be possible in pure energy form. Second, although taking on human form allows us to create on an individual level, it is also a means by which Divine energy can experience through us. That Divine energy does not tell us what to do, nor does it control us or our decisions. Instead, we have complete free will where each being is allowed to make their own choices.

As co-creators, working with Divine energy, there is a responsibility that comes with creation. Everything we think, do, and say goes into forming the collective consciousness—an emotional, mental, spiritual, and mass of energy that influences our way of living our lives. Each individual can influence that collective energy, but the influence of groups or societies can have a far greater impact than the single being. That is why there is more power when people gather together to share beliefs, meditate, or pray.

As co-creators working with the Divine, the guides emphasized that there is responsibility or awareness that comes with creation. We were urged to create in a "noble" way where we "don't make a difference" by hurting, taking, or damaging humanity or the planet. Everything we think, do, and say should be a reflection of the Divine. Those individuals who have embraced a lifestyle focused on wanting, taking, and exploiting for their personal gain are not co-creating with Source.

We have factions of our society that have become enmeshed in negativity, and that energy is manifesting as war, terrorism, cruelty, and abuse. As we—humanity—get angry and despise those individuals, we give them more power and we create a collective consciousness that is filled with anger, fear, and hatred. As a group, if we can come together and envision a world where all individuals are surrounded by love, peace, and light, we have the potential to change the dynamic of our planet.

There were no instances in the dialogues to support the idea that there is some sort of devil or evil entity that is creating this dynamic. It appears that the devil is a man-made invention designed to give negativity a face and perhaps, through fear, control church members who might otherwise go astray from the congregation. Negativity, in which people choose darker life paths, exists. True evil, in the form of an entity or uncontrollable energy, does not.

The guides expressed uncertainty about the future of man and the future of the planet. It appears that this is a situation in flux, and even the guides can't predict that outcome. Perhaps the exact future of the planet is *not* predetermined and truly depends on the free will of the collective population. Fortunately, most of the guides feel that this is a situation that can have a good outcome as the consciousness of the planet elevates to new levels. As Monica's angel, bathed in a blue light, says:

Monica: Yes, the light is being distorted by the darkness of bad choices and the lack of love, so the correction must come from all of us understanding that there is light and there is love in all of those individuals and in all of those situations, and by choosing to connect with that. That is the only way.

We can bring love, light, and forgiveness to the planet if we choose to embrace that state of mindfulness. That *is* the only way.

## A Prayer for a New Consciousness

For those who want to focus on bringing more light to the world, I've included a prayer that provides guidance for how to do that. You can call it a meditation or prayer or visualization—depending on what term feels most comfortable for you—but the objective is the same: to bring more love and light to the world. It can be done by individuals, spiritual groups, or, ideally, by entire congregations in hopes that our vision of positive energy might replace the negative energy that has long been part of our collective consciousness.

As I mentioned earlier, we can't affect anyone's path but our own, so the purpose of this exercise is to continually bring light to all beings in hopes that they might embrace that light and act accordingly. Some may respond to a new consciousness, some may not. If this effort only stops a fraction of the negative energy in the world or only makes one person in a hundred feel more love and connection, then we should be elated that we are changing the course of the planet in a positive way.

Please feel free to insert *God* or *Creator* or *Allah* or *Source* or *Great Spirit* or *Earth energy* or whatever descriptor feels appropriate to your personal belief system each time the word *Divine* is used. The wording can be changed and the prayer can be shortened or reworded; the most important part of any process like this is the intention.

Finally, one of the most important and often neglected elements of prayer is to focus on *feeling* what you want to create. Mere words have little power compared to *feeling* when we work in the realm of manifestation. As you engage in this prayer, try to involve all of your senses because that makes the process much more powerful: imagine what it would feel like if you lived in a world where, at all times, your body and consciousness were completely filled with love and peace, and then allow that warmth to radiate out and connect to the energetic oneness shared by all living things.

# A Prayer for a New Consciousness

### A Prayer of Light

Imagine a beautiful beam of white light coming down from the sky, and you are standing in the middle of that ray of light. It is the light and love and forgiveness of the Divine, and it feels warm and comforting as it surrounds you. Imagine that beam of light filling up your mind and body with peacefulness and brilliance. Embrace that feeling of loving luminescence.

Now imagine expanding the base of that beam of light so it surrounds your entire town, village, or city. Imagine everyone within that light sharing kindness with those in need, reaching out to those who might have lost their way, bringing joy and laughter where there needs to be more illumination, and helping the planet remain lush and full of life.

Now take that white light and imagine wrapping it around the Earth so that the entire planet is immersed in white light. As you do that, there are three large arenas filled with people who also get showered with that white light. The first arena is filled with the lost souls from all over the world, the people who are struggling in life. Perhaps they are unwell or feel alone or depressed or afraid. As this light warmly wraps around each of them, it makes them feel loved and allows them to feel connection, connection to other people and connection to their guidance.

The second arena is filled with all of the governmental and business leaders of the world. There are kings and rulers, presidents and senators. There are CEOs and board members from all of the major corporations. Imagine an abundance of brilliant white light fills this arena and fills their world with love, light, and forgiveness. We have no power over the decisions they make, but with this light, each one has the opportunity to feel that goodness and make decisions that are best for the highest benefit of all mankind.

The third arena holds all of the terrorists and war lords and perpetrators. The light of the Divine saturates each of them with so much love, light, and forgiveness that it is impossible for them to ignore. Our gift to them is brilliance, and each one of them has the opportunity to absorb that light and embrace a new reality.

If you look inside and within this light that illuminates the planet, you might see visions of the future: people putting down their weapons and shaking hands in peace, people giving a helping hand to those in need, people supporting those who might be struggling or feeling despondent, people assisting the animals that walk this planet, and people planting flowers and trees and nurturing the Earth. Take a moment and visualize images that are important to you and what you want to see manifesting with this positive energy. Take a moment and feel your body and heart completely filled with warmth and love.

And now, expand that brilliant light so it fills the entire Universe. Imagine all space, everything, and everyone being filled with peace and love. This is our world now: one of love and light.

Anyone can do this exercise. Each person can be creative and envision this in a manner that feels comfortable to them. Our hope is that by working together we might be able to shift the consciousness of the planet so that positive energy might create a world of love and light.

## Chapter 9

# Understanding the Concept of Time in the Universe

When I started the *One Voice* interviews, I didn't think I needed to include any questions about the concept of time. Like most people, I had come to accept the linear construct of time. We have what we would consider to be concrete evidence of our current belief system because we have all witnessed a linear pattern occurring in our life cycles: people are born, they age, and eventually they die. But as I worked with the guides, they would often allude to the fact that man's concept of time wasn't an accurate portrayal of that dimension. Sometimes the guides would even make statements such as "There is no such thing as time." As these discussions progressed and the guides started sharing information about simultaneous planes and existences, I realized that for us to fully understand

and try to accept those alternative dynamics, we would also have to change our perspective about how time exists in the universe.

In the introductory paragraphs of each chapter, I have tried to share ideas and sometimes include experiences from my life that might support some of alternative ideas presented in this book. My strategy was that if I could unearth and then analyze something in my life that fell in line with the wisdom of the guides, I might be better equipped to understand the dynamic and, in turn, be better able to explain it to others.

With the concept of time this was especially difficult. What evidence could I find in my personal life that might indicate an alternative time construct? I wasn't looking for something that disputed our linear perspective of time. As one guide who compared our multiple existences to being in various "aquariums" put it, linear time is the way time functions in Earth's aquarium. So, what I was looking for was something in my life that suggested there could be an alternative construct of time that might incorporate simultaneous existences.

That became a daunting task because it appears that in this "aquarium" we're not supposed to know much of the information that the guides have graciously shared with us during these interviews. If we came in with such insight, we would simply act on that knowledge and there would be no discovery or learning component to our lives. For example, if an individual had chosen to incarnate with the purpose of coming to peace with their fear of death, how could they learn that lesson if they came in *knowing* that we have thousands of existences and that many of those existences will be shared with members of our soul family? In essence, the solution to the lesson would have already been revealed and that awareness would probably interfere with their learning and their potential to evolve.

So, is this information, the revelations in this book, providing us with forbidden material? I don't think so. Perhaps more information is being given because the Earth and humanity have reached a point where we desperately need guidance. Ultimately, I believe that if an individual can establish an authentic connection with Divine energy, they are opening doors for communication to be shared that can help them on their journey. The problem is that, until recently, our society has not encouraged us to pursue that *individualized* spiritual path because of institutional interference and control.

I found myself trying to rally against traditional societal beliefs in an attempt to come up with some sort of indication that a completely different time construct actually exists. That created a challenge. I tried to look back through my lifetime to see if I had any experiences that might suggest a possible variation on the notion of time that didn't fall in line with our widely accepted linear theory.

I knew I needed to consider looking at this topic from an innovative perspective. If my approach was to be rational or logical, it would merely duplicate the methods man has taken for centuries, where our "knowledge" was based on science and religion. To understand the dimension of time in a way that falls outside of those disciplines meant that I had to throw out what we deem to be scientific "truth" and consider alternative ideas.

With this new set of ground rules in place, I eventually came up with something from my life that I thought might challenge our traditional perspectives about time. It involved recurring dreams I have had throughout my life. In these dreams, the subject matter can and does change, but the setting is *always* the same. These dreams all take place at my childhood home, the place I lived from ages 1 through 12. About once a week I have one of those dreams that take me back there, and that occurrence has been consistent regardless of where I have lived or what issues have been present in my life. I have returned to that same location thousands of times. It seems odd that I go back to that same setting on such a regular basis, especially in a world in which there are no coincidences.

It is very rare for me to dream about other places I've lived, so why do I go back so frequently to this site of my formative years, and how might these visits to my childhood home be connected to the concept of time? During the *One Voice* sessions, many guides had talked about how we do work on other levels and possibly even move to other dimensions in our sleep. With that in mind, I wondered if there was something in my dream location that might be a portal to other planes. If we accept the premise that there are parallel planes of existence, perhaps I return to that childhood home to enter a door or opening that would take me into these other worlds or other planes. And when I mention this, I'm not trying to imply that this is something *only* I do or that there is something special about me. Perhaps this is a common occurrence for all of our spirits to move between planes during our sleep. Perhaps that is one of the nonphysical purposes of sleep. It might be that this is the location of *my* gateway, but perhaps others use different gateways. There might even be a mind-blocking element to this form of travel in which we don't wake up remembering the dream that identifies the location of the portal, nor do we remember the experience each time we enter into those other dimensions. It might be similar to how we don't readily or consciously remember such things as past lives or where our soul was prior to this incarnation.

That was my initial thought: there are concurrent planes of time, and I am leaving this world through a portal that helps me connect to other tentacles of my amoebic soul that exist in these other worlds. It's pretty far out, but remember: if I limit my introspection to rational thought and documented "evidence," then there is no possibility of new concepts coming into our consciousness and no ability to expand our thinking.

But I mentioned that my understanding of time was a work in progress. The portal concept was only the beginning of this expanded thinking. After completing the chapter about soul families (Chapter 4), another possibility came to me. When I return home in these dreams, I often see members of my childhood family. Sometimes they are the same age that they were when I was growing up. Sometimes, they are older. Assuming these are people who are part of my soul family—some still living in a physical body on this planet and some deceased—I started to wonder if this might be my way of connecting with my soul family. Perhaps we share experiences or check in for guidance with this group of people who we are eternally close to and with whom we often reincarnate. Because we are being told "there is no time"—at least in the way that humans think about it—this could be a location where my soul family convenes to share knowledge and reconnect as we check in from our many different dimensions.

So, this was my starting point in an effort to gain a new understanding of time. As I learned more in these conversations, I've tried to share that information and my impressions; however, I knew this was going to be a difficult subject because whenever the concept of time came up, the most common response from the guides was that time was one of those paradigms that the human mind cannot fully comprehend.

As I mentioned at the beginning of this chapter, our conventional model of time needed to be refined because of the fact that parallel or simultaneous planes had come up so often in these dialogues. I wondered how we could be present in concurrent planes when our Earth experience, by all appearances, does not support that possibility. That is how the element of time came into the conversation with Heather who was working with Archangel Raphael.

JS: Are we in multiple places at one time? In other words, is there just this one Earth's existence or are we present in different existences at the same time?

Heather: There are multiple nows that exist, since time is not linear. There are many moments that exist at the same time.

JS: Can you explain the concept of time not being linear? Our perspective is that it is linear. How is time really functioning?

Heather: Everything is in one moment. Everything is in one particular point. All things and all existence, and all, exist at one moment. It's very difficult to explain because of the way your brain patterns look at time.

JS: So at the same time that I'm sitting here right now asking these questions, I could be a 10-year-old playing football in the park?

As I was growing up, one of my passions was playing football with my friends. I asked this question because I was trying to get clarification that even within *this life* we are in multiple places. In other words, at the same time as I write this book, I am also in my 20s driving through that pounding rainstorm on Highway 101, and I am a 10-year-old playing football with my friends.

Heather: Yes.

JS: And I could be a being on another planet at the same time as well?

Heather: You are, yes.

Despite the fact that this exchange is a perfect opportunity for my detractors to insert their alien jokes, the important takeaway is that we are in multiple places at the same time, a dynamic that would be impossible with our current beliefs about time. That concept, of "everything is in one moment," came up in many of these conversations. Everything is happening simultaneously. Our logical "brain patterns" want to conceptualize it as one existence coming after the next, but that is not what is being conveyed.

JS: So, there is no time?

Heather: Correct.

JS: It's all happening in, you said, a single moment?

Heather: Yes.

JS: So, when we come on to this planet, we get the appearance of time through the aging process.

Heather: Yes.

JS: Why is that? Is it because we believe in that?

Heather: It serves. It serves many lessons. Part of it is the density, the actual energy of the planet, the density that you experience, illness, and aging, and degradation in your bodies.

The answer about why we become older and live in a linear construct during our time on this planet comes back to one of the most important reasons for our existence: "It serves many lessons." Part of our aging comes with the "density" of being in a physical body, and the experience of aging provides an opportunity for us to learn our lessons, especially about compassion and empathy.

Phil, working with Source, explains why we need to age in this "aquarium" and how the changes we undergo can help facilitate our learning.

JS: When we're worried about getting older in this lifetime, Source might look at that and say, "What's the big issue; this is just a little blip in time. Don't worry about it because there's so much more you're going to learn and experience."

Phil: You're right. You're right, but Source also wants you to experience being old, wants you to feel the aches and pains because that's how you grow in compassion. If we all died at 30, nobody would ever understand what it is to lose energy, vibrancy, maybe even lose your memories, and then come out on the other side with all of it back again.

The linear dynamic on this planet helps facilitate our learning. Through elements such as physical and emotional pain, infirmity, aging, and mortality, we learn how to love and how to feel compassion and empathy. It also provides a framework in which to observe that there are consequences to each of our actions. Our aging minds and emotions give us the opportunity to expand the depth of our life experience. When we exist in spirit form—where our soul is pure energy—it might be impossible, in that state, to feel what it is like to be physically or mentally impaired, what it is like to grow old, or to even feel remorse for our actions. That is how the human existence and physical embodiment can facilitate learning, but linear time is needed for that to happen. Sometimes the child who makes fun of the old man struggling to walk with his cane needs to eventually become the old man with a cane in order to understand what that feels like.

> JS: You've described other existences—other planets, planes, universes—is this a linear thing where we experience these one at a time, or are we having multiple experiences at the same time?

> Phil: There is no time. Everything is happening now. There is no tomorrow; there's no yesterday. It's [that view is] only from our [human] perspective. To answer your question, yes, all of these experiences are happening simultaneously, but they never end either. It's sometimes difficult for our mind to wrap around eternity. We can think sometimes about always being, but we can't really imagine that we've always been, and that's what people don't understand.

Once again, we are told, these experiences are "happening simultaneously, but they never end either." All existence is simultaneous. Our souls don't die; they are alive for "eternity." There is no endpoint. We keep growing and evolving.

It is interesting that the guides of two people who have never met—Heather and Phil—can provide such similar information, especially when it falls outside of rational human thinking. From what I know of these two clients, it is doubtful that these answers would have come from their conscious minds. There is a good chance that neither would agree, in full, with these perspectives, and yet, it is interesting that there are so many similarities. Both passages tell us that we need to go through the aging process on Earth in order to learn our lessons. Both tell us that these concepts are very difficult for our human minds to understand. Both tell us there are simultaneous planes of existence and "everything is happening now." But how can it be that we are in multiple places—even within our present existence on Earth—at the same time?

I asked Sarah's group of guides (led by her master guide) that question: how we can be in two places at the same time. Sarah was one of many clients who were able to go with their guides and experience what it was like to be on another plane. When her master guide took her to visit one of the otherworldly dimensions where her energy concurrently resides, a place she described as "a starry existence," I wanted to know how this was possible.

JS: How can a soul be here on Earth and on another plane, such as the starry existence [which she had described earlier in the session], at the same time? It's hard for our human minds understand this?

Sarah: He [Sarah's guide] is in the room, but he's also the stars. He's in both places at once. [Sarah talks directly to him.] How do you do that? I don't know. [Then she talks to me again.] He's showing his body in both places, but you can see it's blurred because he's moving really fast between the two. Maybe it's not simultaneous, it's blurred.

JS: For brief moments you can check out and be in the other place? You can switch back and forth really fast?

Sarah: Yeah. Right.

JS: Is this our soul or spirit that's in all these different places? What should we call that?

Sarah: Yeah, I guess it's our soul.

JS: It must be that our soul has several pieces?

Sarah: The soul has pieces, yeah. He's conscious of being in both places. It kind of reminds me of like an atom splitting. They've learned… [Her train of thought changes in mid-sentence in order to provide an example.] You know how this couch [as she touches the chair beneath her] is not really solid, we just see it that way. He is saying they've learned how to do that, split the atoms.

Despite past resistance from the scientific community, it has now been proven that everything in our world is, in fact, made up of energy. The couch "is not really solid," because it is made up of energy.

Humans are also made up of energy and that energy can split and be present in various forms. Our essence can separate into different manifestations. We can be in multiple places at the same time. We are not our physical bodies; we are spiritual essence.

As I pursued the question of how we could be in multiple places at once, an interesting phenomenon occurred with Caitlyn. Caitlyn was communicating with a group of guides that was led by Archangel Michael, but when I started asking questions about time, another presence came in, but this guidance came *through* her instead of appearing as an external being. It started when Caitlyn couldn't get an answer to one of the questions. It was as if her guide suddenly became silent.

Caitlyn: He's not telling me anything.

Archangel Michael suddenly stopped answering questions. Then, after a pause, she continued.

Caitlyn: It's almost like I'm channeled.
JS: What do you mean by that?
Caitlyn: Well, it's me, but it's coming from somewhere else. It's like ancient me.
JS: Can this ancient you channel the answers?
Caitlyn: Yeah, sort of. It's like a knowing that's always been there. It's like I'm old, so old.

One of the fascinating things about this work is the guides were always answering questions on different levels. I would often go back and revisit answers only to find remarkable discoveries in the subtext. In this case, as we were talking about simultaneous existences, another version or soul part of Caitlyn came right into her body. It is as if the guides wanted to give us evidence of simultaneous dimensions and show us that we can move from one dimension to another by having that phenomenon actually occur during the interview.

Because this was something Caitlyn had never experienced before, I asked her if she was comfortable with this other part of her coming inside her body.

> JS: Is it okay for your old soul to channel?
>
> Caitlyn: Yes.
>
> JS: We talked about essence, and how we are essence, in different existences. Are these existences happening at the same time or is it linear? We think of our lives as being linear. Are we in more than one place at once?
>
> Caitlyn: We travel.

Here was an occurrence of a soul part truly traveling.

> JS: Tell me about that.
>
> Caitlyn: We go to other places to learn at night, in the dream state.

This certainly wasn't the first time one of the guides had mentioned the work we do "in the dream state," but it was especially pertinent given the assertion I made about traveling in my sleep at the beginning of this chapter.

> JS: So we are not just in one place at one time?
>
> Caitlyn: No.
>
> JS: So this old soul of Caitlyn's is from some other plane right now?
>
> Caitlyn: Um-hm, yeah.

To provide evidence of the simultaneous nature of the Universe, a part of Caitlyn came from another dimension and channeled through her. That is different from the guides that some of the clients have channeled while participating in this project. The difference is that this one was a being that shared the same soul or higher self as Caitlyn. In the other cases where a client channeled, it was *not* a being who shared the same spiritual identity. The implication of this ancient part coming forward is that it presented a dynamic that supports the theory of simultaneous existences. If this had been a guide that was unknown to Caitlyn, the message would not have been as convincing as when a soul part comes directly through the subject.

JS: We talked about how we can be in two places at once. Is time linear or is this all happening at once?

Caitlyn: There is no time. There is no time. No time.

JS: Then time is a man-made thing?

Caitlyn: Yes.

JS: But we get older which gives as the illusion of time.

Caitlyn: What did you say? It's an illusion? No, it's real here.

JS: So, when you say there is no time, can you talk about that?

Caitlyn: There's time here. On other planes it's not important. It doesn't exist.

Time is "real here," on the Earth plane, but not in the bigger picture. Again, we need to age on this planet because of the knowledge that comes with that development.

To get a better understanding of why linear time and aging occur on Earth but not on other planes, I asked Zeb, who was working with his guardian angel, for clarity on these contrasting dynamics. As I mentioned earlier, there are many descriptors people use for Divine energy. With Zeb, the descriptor was God.

JS: We talked about different incarnations. It sounds like there are different planes or levels or multiple existences available to us. Am I saying that right?

Zeb: Yes.

JS: Are these different existences, in some cases, happening simultaneously?

Zeb: Always.

JS: I'm trying to understand the concept of time because humans look at time as being linear. We start at point A and end at point B, but I get a sense that is not accurate. In the bigger picture, it may not be linear. Can you explain time in a way that us humans might understand how it works?

This was the origin of the aquarium references I've used in this chapter.

Zeb: The simplest way that I can explain it is like, God likes collecting beautiful fishes, and there are these aquariums, and each aquarium is very different, and each aquarium is within its own tank. Now some aquariums might have salt water, some might have fresh, and some may not have water at all because they are in something that He can interchange for water. And these different tanks do connect to each other, and when they connect they become a sphere if you will, but each of them are individual, but yet they are still one because He created them. He can either go inside each of them or just view them or create more. So, within these different tanks there are different lives that go on and they create on their own.

It is as if these different aquariums represent separate, but simultaneous, planes of existence and we might be within multiple aquariums at the same time. Each aquarium has its own set of rules. For example, our aquarium has linear time, but other aquariums might have a different time construct. The assertion that God or the Divine can go inside or view these tanks supports the contention that the Divine experiences through us, but does not interfere with our paths. We are in charge of our own life direction, as reflected in the statement "There are different lives that go on and they create on their own," emphasizing the fact that we have free will, a point that was made in Chapter 5 about our life lessons. We determine what we create or how we want our lives to take shape.

JS: Are you saying that energy, like a spirit or soul, could be in all these different fish at same time?

Zeb: Yeah.

JS: Are there really hundreds of millions of years that go by or is that a man-made concept?

Zeb: In this particular aquarium [Earth] it's a perfect concept, but in another aquarium, it could be something totally different. Each one of them creates its own.

JS: So humans [in our aquarium] could have hundreds of millions of years, but if we were on another plane of existence it may be...

Zeb [interrupting]: Seconds.

JS: It could be seconds?

Zeb: Nano seconds. The blink of an eye. People realize that when they look inwards that they can be many places at once.

Apparently, the rules governing Earth's aquarium include time operating in a linear fashion, but within the multitudes of other "aquariums" different sets of rules may apply. Once again, if we look at the bigger picture of the entire Universe, there continues to be the notion that all action and events are happening simultaneously or in "nano seconds."

I was intrigued by this comment: "People realize that when they look inwards that they can be many places at once." It implies that we have the capability of exploring these other planes that are happening simultaneously with our current lives. I wanted to know more about our multidimensional nature and see if that was true. I explored this concept with Loraine's guides, which included a bear, an angel, a fairy, and a young girl spirit guide. In my question, I was wondering if everything in our lives is happening at the same time. In other words, as Loraine is presently in my office, is it possible she is simultaneously experiencing life as a young girl and as an elderly woman?

> JS: So, Loraine is here now, but there's a part of her that might be 30 years old doing things at the same time as she is here now, and there's a part of her who might be 7 years old doing things at the same time and a part of her that might be 85 and doing things at the same time.
>
> Loraine: Yes. Yes.

What I was asking was if our various experiences on *this* planet, in *this* life, are all happening at the same time. Loraine's guides said they were.

As a hypnotherapist, this is not surprising because in our practices we commonly use a process called age regression in which, in hypnosis, clients go back to different moments in their current life. The purpose of that technique is to help clients release or forgive or process past events that might be interfering with their well-being at the present time. When clients go back to earlier times in their life, it can often feel like they are actually there, reliving that moment, a phenomenon known as revivification. Through that revivification experience, it is not uncommon for the retrieval to be quite remarkable. I remember, when I first started practicing, conducting a regression with a woman who was in her late 60s. She went back to a time where she had her first cigarette. She was with a group of friends in the bathroom at her junior high school. Not only could she lucidly describe each of the friends who were there, but she went on to talk about the ugly, greenish gray paint on the walls and even the number of holes in the ceiling tiles. (This was back in the days when ceilings were covered with square acoustical tiles and each square had a configuration of holes, perhaps a pattern of 24 holes × 24 holes on each tile.) After many years of listening to my clients recall specific details, such as the memory described by that smoking cessation client, it raised the question of whether those experiences could be actually happening concurrently with every other event in our lives. After all, the guides keep saying that everything is happening at once.

As I further investigated the contention that everything is happening now, I wondered if events from other lives—which we regard as history—could also be occurring concurrently with our present lives, as this possibility came up earlier in Chapter 3. Could we be in different lives at the same time we are here now? I asked Loraine's guides.

JS: We have what we call history here, but you're telling me everything is concurrent. Loraine is here in this chair right now, but could she, at the same time as she is here, also be a farmer in New England in the 1800s? And could she also be a scholar who is living in Greece in the antiquities? Is she in all these different planes and levels or is she just in one place at once?

Loraine: Many different planes, and levels. Many different lifetimes, yes. But the focus and the awareness and the concentration is in this body right now.

JS: Why isn't the focus in the body of the farmer in the 1800s? Why is she more focused here and not in one of those other existences?

Loraine: There is a way of being in this body concurrently with whatever was in the past and whatever is in the future. This is the place of remembering right now.

JS: If Loraine wanted a glimpse of one of those other existences, if she wanted for a moment to tune into another existence, could she do that?

Loraine: Yes.

I had Loraine go through a series of steps so she could go to another of her concurrent experiences. In this case, we were accessing a "past life" with the idea of exploring whether it really is a past or a concurrent life. It took Loraine a few moments to respond. It was as if she were scanning many possibilities.

> Loraine: There are so many [lives]; I don't know which one to pick. [She pauses.] Okay. I'm a maiden. It looks like a long dress, buckets of water, old dirt road, long hair, braided. I'm a peasant, hard work, not an easy life, unhappy.

Notice the difference in the manner of speech between Loraine's comments as the peasant compared to the patterns of speech expressed when she is relaying information from her guides. These kinds of variations are common in regressions and suggest that there truly is a different voice and different personality coming through.

After that experience, I asked Loraine to come back to the present and talk about that life time.

> Loraine [crying]: I feel sad.
>
> JS: For her [the maiden]?
>
> Loraine: Yeah.
>
> JS: And guides, should she feel sad? Or is there learning or lessons in that existence?
>
> Loraine: It is very necessary to learn. It is connected to now.

The words "it is connected to now" tell us that all of these existences, though appearing to be worlds apart, may, in fact, be quite interconnected and perhaps even simultaneous. They are not separate because the soul part in each existence is interconnected.

> JS: Guides, I've only asked about this plane, but are there other existences, other dimensions?
>
> Loraine: Ah, yes. Yes.

I asked Loraine if she wanted to experience one of those other dimensions outside of the plane of ordinary human existence. She said she did, so we went through a process that enabled her to visit another plane and then came back. This was her observation after she returned.

> Loraine: There's a place to explore that is out beyond the crown chakra. It's out beyond, but it's still part of this physical—it's not physical—a golden rope that connects us to a place out beyond our head. And it's expansive and that's where all of our contracts for this lifetime are concluded and defined.

During that visit to this other realm, I had Loraine look at one of her contracts that revealed information that was personal to her and relevant to her present journey.

Throughout this book, several clients have ventured into other dimensions. Loraine experienced another realm and also participated in what we commonly refer to as a past life regression. But based on the information that we are learning about time, that nomenclature, *past life regression*, might be misleading because what we call past lives might actually be occurring at the same time we are going through our present lives.

It is fairly easy for clients to experience age regressions and past life regressions. Movement to simultaneous existences on other planes is definitely more difficult, but is important to our new understanding of time because it helps us begin to see how many dimensions we can inhabit simultaneously. In the next series of regressions with Shelly, working with her spirit guide and an animal guide, I began by asking if she would be willing to explore the idea that her spirit energy might be present in another realm, at the same time it is with us right now on planet Earth.

> JS: Could we allow Shelly to get just a glimpse of what another dimension might look like, in which her energy might be at the same time as she is here now?

I wanted to get permission from both Shelly and her guides before we began the process. All parties gave their consent, so we went through the process, and then I checked in with Shelly.

> JS: You might just get a quick glimpse of an image of what it's like in this other dimension.
>
> Shelly [takes a long, deep breath]: Like crystals. It reminds me of—I haven't seen *Superman* for a long time—like those longer white crystals, and they're just kind of everywhere. I don't want to say that it feels cold because it doesn't feel cold, but it's just beautiful. [Her voice becomes very relaxed.] It's peaceful.

Due to the fact that some of the images clients observe in other realms are often quite fantastical, it isn't uncommon for those individuals to compare those visions to things they had seen in the movies because that is the only place where they've been exposed to otherworldly representations.

> JS: Is this a place that you are concurrently with where you are now? In other words, is part of your energy in this space and part of your energy on the Earth right now?
>
> Shelly: Yes.

I had her come back to the present time and then asked her about the experience.

> JS: Based on what we just experienced, it sounds like we're in more than one place at one time?
>
> Shelly: Um-hm.

In Chapter 3, other clients visited other dimensions. I wanted to confirm that those existences are concurrent with where they are now.

The next question I wanted to investigate, to get a better understanding of time, was that if our souls are truly fragmented into parallel existences, could we explore what other lives we might be having concurrently on Earth. In other words, could we get a glimpse of what other physical bodies on this planet our soul might inhabit at the very same moment that we are in the here and now? Perhaps this could be called "parallel life regressions." I wanted to see if it was feasible that Shelly's energy was not only in my office, but also within other humans on this planet.

JS: So, is it possible that Shelly is not just here in this chair, but at the same time her higher self energy might be a farmer in the Philippines or she might be a teacher in India? Is it possible that she's not just here, but her higher self energy might be in a few other individuals on this planet? Is that possible?

After that initial question received affirmation, I then posed the question directly to Shelly.

JS: If your energy is in someone else at this time, could you get a glimpse of what that existence is like, and would you be willing to do that?

Shelly: Yes.

JS: And would they [her guides] be willing to let you?

Shelly: Yes.

JS: This would be another body that you inhabit on Earth at the same time as you're here now. And tell me what you see?

Shelly: I'm like in a grandmother. I feel like my feet are in water, but I'm working. I'm pulling something like some sort of a plant. I want to say like rice paddies, but it's very wet. My feet are very wet, and I've got a wrap around my head for protection from sun. But I'm old and hunched over, but peaceful.

JS: Is there anything about that energy that feels familiar or does it seem like a totally different experience?

Shelly: It seems like there's something familiar about it, but I know I've never done it. Shelly [referring to herself in the third person] has never done that.

Wanting more evidence, I asked Shelly if it would be okay for us to explore the possibility that there might be other concurrent lives on this planet.

JS: Would it be okay for us to look at another life to see where else your spirit might be at this time? This is, again, a concurrent lifetime. It is a glimpse of where you might be at the same time you are here now.

Shelly: I see a tiger.

JS: You're in a tiger or you see a tiger?

I wanted to clarify.

Shelly: I see a tiger, but I feel close to the tiger. I'm not afraid of the tiger. I can cuddle the tiger. I can be with the tiger, but I don't think I'm at a zoo, but I'm inside somewhere that is designed to look like the rainforest or the jungle, but it's definitely inside.

JS: Are you a person?

Shelly: I think so, but I can't see myself. I can only see the tiger. I just feel a lot of love for the tiger.

JS: So you aren't sure if you are a person or an animal?

Shelly: Yeah.

JS: Could your energy be in an animal at the same time as it is inside you?

Shelly: I think it could be.

Earlier in this book, it was established that Divine energy is in all of us. There is the possibility that Shelly's visions, during this work, may simply be her tapping into Divine energy and going places where the Divine is present, which is within everything. However, during these regressions, I was trying to get Shelly to look at where her *unique* energy was inhabiting other life forms. I was specifically asking for examples where her higher self energy was residing within other life forms. I say life forms because this experience brought up the question of whether our energy might also reside within animals.

> JS: What does that tell you about our connection to the Earth and to animals?
>
> Shelly: It's beautiful. They're so much more elevated than we are. They only want peace.

It wasn't clear if Shelly's energy was inside the animal or someone who felt a strong connection to that animal. Either way, it indicates the multidimensional nature of our energy. I wanted another example of Shelly being within another human body, so I asked her to explore that possibility.

> JS: Let's check in on one more existence, another existence or place where your spirit energy or higher self is at the same time as it is here right now.

After a few moments, Shelly described another reality.

> Shelly: I see a native, but in the cold areas, wearing white fur, whitish and grayish fur around the legs. It's a man, kind of bare-chested. I think I'm the man.
>
> JS: What is that like?
>
> Shelly: I feel the strength, and the word that's coming up is pride, stoic.

JS: Do you get a sense of where this would be? What part of the world?

Shelly: I want to say someplace cold like Canada or Alaska.

JS: And does anything about that world seem a little bit familiar or does it seem very strange?

Shelly: No, it feels familiar.

JS: What does this tell you about our energy?

Shelly: That it's fluid.

JS: Is it in a lot of places at one time?

Shelly: Yeah, not contained.

JS: Not just in one person?

Shelly: No.

JS: Why does it seem that way? And this is a question for the guides: why do we only have an awareness of being here and now in this body?

Shelly: Because we've created that restraint. We've created that illusion. It's just that, an illusion.

Linear time, as a guide said earlier in this chapter, is not an illusion, but "We've created that restraint," in which part of our belief system—the perception that we can only be in one place at a time—*is* an illusion.

I asked Shelly what it was like to have an awareness of how it feels to be in touch with her energy when that energy is present in so many dimensions.

Shelly: It's like being the ether, being the air, and being the light too. And right now I feel all that energy trapped in my body because that's what I've come to believe, that that energy is just within me, and I've been holding onto it.

JS: Is it bad? Do you need to do something with it?

Shelly: No, I think they're just trying to show me how we see ourselves—we are just the skin—almost like a balloon, but we think that we can hold it all in. Our purpose is to expand and to share it, not to withhold it.

JS: To expand and share the light?

Shelly: Um-hm, and the energy. Whatever the energy exchange is: love, light, peace.

JS: So, based on what you're telling me, we are in more than one place at one time?

Shelly: Um-hm.

JS: But what about what we refer to as a past life, is that—and I'm asking your guides—in the past, or is it also happening at the same time as we are in the here in now?

Shelly: They're showing me books with the pages kind of separated, like there's air between them, like parallel universes happening at the same time, but they're all in the same book.

JS: Does that mean that they're all happening at the same time?

Shelly: That's what it feels like.

JS: So if we went back to a past life, if you're willing to do that, what is a past life that you are living at the same time that you are here right now? If you're willing to go and your guides will take you, let's look for a past life that is happening at the same time that you here now.

We took a moment to set up the next regression.

Shelly: I'm seeing a young Native woman. I can't tell if she's from the same time and space as the man [referring to the Native man from the current life regression mentioned above].

JS: Is this the colder climate, similar to what you spoke of earlier, or a different setting?

Shelly: I can't tell. It feels like it's different. I don't see the fur.

JS: Is there something familiar about her?

Shelly: There's something very familiar about her.

JS: What is her journey in this particular incarnation? What is she learning or figuring out? What is her lesson?

Shelly: How to be by herself. How to be with herself.

JS: And why is that important?

Shelly: So that she can feel peace.

JS: Does this relate to any of your lessons?

Without hesitation, Shelly shared a personal experience from her current life that represented that exact same lesson. I had Shelly come back to the present time.

JS: Once again, this was a past life, but, in a sense, was that life happening at the same time as this one? Is that what you are getting?

Shelly: Yeah.

JS: What do you think about that?

Shelly: It's weird. I was not expecting that.

JS: I want to ask your guides, if we went back in time to time when Shelly was a young girl, to a good time, maybe when she was playing with a friend, and [to Shelly] if you will allow a scene like that to formulate in your mind.

Shelly [confirming that she was able to bring up a scene that fits that description]: Um-hm.

JS: Is that scene happening now at the same time you are here or is that scene really in the past?

Shelly: The scene feels like it's in the past.

JS: What do your guides say?

Shelly: They say it's now. [She pauses.] I think, I think it's in the past because I see myself as a young girl.

JS [to her guides]: We have this idea about linear time on this planet. Is time really linear, or are all of these things happening at the same time? What do your guides say?

Shelly: It's happening at the same time. It's circular.

JS [to Shelly]: And what did you think about this topic before you sat in this chair?

Shelly: I feel like I've lived a lineal life, but I've been trying to see it more cosmically. They showed me a circle and my essence was like a ball of energy in the center, and everything in that circle just went right into the center. Maybe that's my soul, but it's expanded into all of this around it, all of these things happening at the same time.

It is interesting that these images of the ball of energy foreshadow the description of the time construct that is yet to come in the last part of this chapter, despite the fact that the information comes from two different clients working with very different guides.

JS: So, when we look at what we call past lives, we look at things happening in this life, we look at how our higher self or soul or spirit could be in other dimensions or other bodies, is everything happening all at the same time? Is it all happening now?

Shelly: Yes.

JS: Guides, why is this happening, because human minds don't get this? Can you explain this to us?

Shelly: It's because we have a false belief about time. Time is like different dimensions.

JS: What do you mean by that?

Shelly: When you think of those things that happened in the past, it's just going to a different dimension of who you are, like an internal realm, and when you have those déjà vu moments, those are things that are actual things that are going to happen, like you're traveling to another dimension. I don't want to say future, but it's like what's there, what's available.

Think about how many times people recall past events and say: "That feels like it was from a different lifetime." Perhaps, instead, it is from a different dimension. This would explain those moments when we experience déjà vu. It would make sense that we could see glimpses of the future because the future is essentially happening now. We are simultaneously experiencing the future just like we are simultaneously experiencing the past.

JS: If all this is correct, this would mean that Shelly could go to something in the future and see that too, if she is willing. It could even be a week or two from now.

After taking a moment to allow the images to come forth, this was the response:

Shelly: I'm in my classroom.

JS: Are you teaching?

Shelly: I am. I am standing in front of them, but I am not teaching at the board. It's like a conversation. I've just met these students. I see faces, but I honestly don't know if they are my students, but I know the room.

JS: So this could be next semester?

Shelly: Or even next week because I just started the semester. So the room is very familiar. I know what room and I know what class it would be.

These journeys into the past, present, and future give us a sense of the simultaneous nature of our multidimensional universe. Shelly was able to experience a past life as a Native woman, another time—as a young girl—during her present life, a future scene in this life, and a couple of concurrent existences where she was in other earthly bodies. Additionally, she was able to visit another realm. How could this be possible? That was the next step: trying to conceptualize a new time construct in a way that our human minds could understand it.

I started asking the guides to describe the dimension of time in a way in which we could assemble a conceptual model that would make sense to the human brain. As these dialogues progressed, it became more difficult because that model needed to include a universe with simultaneous existences where everything, despite the appearance of linear time, was actually happening in the now. Naturally, the image needed to come from the guides, even though many of them said that the concept was going to be very difficult for human minds to fully understand. One of the clearest descriptions came from Margaret's spirit guide.

JS: What about the concept of time? I'm trying to come up with a way to explain it. What I hear from the guides and angels is that man's concept of time is a linear construct—we are born, we age, and we die—and so we think of it in linear terms. But what I'm being told is that is not the case. Is there a way you can explain it in human terms so we can understand about time?

Margaret: If we could remove ourselves from the Earth and go to the higher self in a conscious manner, so that we could do it and remember, we would see all experiences in every dimension are present now. It's as if we are inside, we are in space maybe as a point of light [under her breath], no that's too small. Our higher self is a source of energy. The energy is light and it is also not light. It is what we would call dark matter. We are everything, always now, within the experiences that we are having. So we are as an entity in space creating energy, supporting our linear experiences. I don't have something on Earth to compare this to.

The guide tells us that if we could view this dynamic from the perspective of our higher self, we would see that "all experiences in every dimension are present now." Based on our earthly experiences, we want to insist that there is a progression of events that create our dynamic of time, but that notion in these dialogues has been challenged on numerous occasions. Even though Margaret's guide says "I don't have something on Earth to compare this to," the guide does describe a model that was one of the easiest to grasp.

> Margaret: If you are a power station—you know when you drive down a highway and you see a large power station? Our higher self is much like a large conscious power station. The higher self is having many experiences, has many powerlines going out to many places at the same time. Only our powerlines, we act as something like a very flexible arm, and at the end of the arm, instead of hand, there is a ball of light. That ball of light is the entity in that dimension, in that moment having that experience. The measure of time doesn't exist from the point of view of the highest self. We are only in this moment having this experience, whichever one that is, of all the experiences we may be having. It could be 20. It could be hundreds. It could be thousands for some beings of higher self. It could maybe be thousands of experiences happening at one time. A normal amount would be 100, maybe a hundred experiences happening at one time. In order to gain information, we provide energy to our extensions and we take information in from the extensions.

Using the broadcasting tower example, each of our higher selves is like a power station. We send out light or energy to hundreds if not thousands of "places." Each of those places could be a different dimension or lifetime when you look at this from a larger, Universal perspective. Our power lines are like "flexible arms" and "at the end of the arm, instead of hand, there is a ball of light. That ball of light is the entity in that dimension, in that moment having that experience." Those places of light can be in different manifestations on Earth, whether that be "past lives," such as the peasant woman described by Loraine, or present concurrent lives, such as the elderly woman working in the rice paddies described by Shelly. In other words, our energy can be present in all of those places and multiple experiences at once.

The image of balls of energy at the end of each arm suggests that there is life in each of those manifestations. It is not just power being delivered to a location; it is power—from the higher self—that is the energy going to the entity or being, that is us, in that dimension. This energy is concurrently being delivered to multiple planes within our present life. For example, one of those balls of energy might be going to the hospital lighting us up as a newborn; another might be going to our elementary school, where we are nervously standing in front of the class; another might be lighting us up while we sit at the dinner table of our childhood home, and so on. In other words, there is a continuous current, but also simultaneous currents.

On a grander scale, one of those balls of energy might be on this planet in this time, another might be 100 years ago, and another might be 100 years in the future, and so on. Those existences may appear to be centuries apart, but they are actually all happening simultaneously but in different aquariums. And if we expand this farther, perhaps some of those powerlines and balls of energy are light beings or spirit guides or energy forms occurring within that starry existence that some have described earlier in this book when they visited other planes.

In each of these manifestations, the light energy is moving back and forth from each of these planes and reconnecting with the power station which is our higher self. As the spirit guide says, "we provide energy to our extensions and we take information in from the extensions." The energy flows to and from our higher self.

As the discussion with Margaret's guide progressed, I mistakenly referred to a radio broadcast tower instead of a power station and the guide quickly corrected me because that wasn't consistent with the comparison.

JS: If we talk about it like a radio tower broadcasting a radio signal and that radio signal might reach 1,000 houses, but instead of the signal it is more like a ball of the energy or our existence is in all of these 1,000 houses.

Margaret: Yes, that's a good picture of what happens, but it's more on the level of energy. Radio is broadcast. What we are doing is conscious, so it's much more analogous to electrical line going to one house. It's directed and conscious, our efforts are conscious. They're not scattered as in a broadcast.

JS: And those houses, instead of all being on Earth, could be on all different planes and different dimensions?

Margaret: Yes.

This model helped me get a better visual of the dynamics of time and consciousness. We started with that amoebic soul image with arms or tentacles that stretched out into other existences. Then there was the mention of fractionation and how we could exist on various realms because energy can be in multiple places at the same time. All of those analogies were very helpful, but perhaps the power station model, at least for me, became the easiest way to understand and visualize the multidimensional nature of our souls.

With a conceptual model in place, I returned to the conjecture from the beginning of this chapter about the significance of my dreams. I asked some of the guides what, if any, significance those dreams may serve. I explained the recurring location of those dreams, but did *not* share any of the specifics of my theories about why I believe that phenomenon occurs. This was the reply from Loraine's guides.

Loraine: As far as going back in the dream state, there are things that are being untangled in your personality. It's like...why?

[Mumbles, as if she is getting clarification.] It's as if that's a doorway for you to have a point of reference for your new place in life now. Do you want to stop going back?

JS: No, I actually enjoy it. It is settling, grounding.

Loraine: And that's why you choose to go back. It's a doorway. I see it as an image of a threshold, a doorway, and you get to choose whether you go back or not. You could easily not. You could decide.

JS: So, this location may be a portal or gateway where I can go and check in with myself on other planes, other existences, other worlds.

Loraine: Yes, exactly, exactly. It's a good place for you.

JS: So it is sort of a gateway?

Loraine: Portal is a good word for that. Yes.

When I asked Margaret's guide the same question about the dreams, the response came with no hesitation, but the answer was different.

Margaret [interrupting my question]: You met someone there.

JS: What you mean?

Margaret: Probably, in your words, more as a place to get guidance. Not a portal specifically. Someone meets you there. Someone who teaches you, your guide, someone from another dimension that you have access to meet you there.

JS: And that's my reason for going there, get the information, get the guidance, and to work with that person?

Margaret: Yes, yes.

The first guidance mentioned the portal. The second one said it was for guidance. On the surface it may appear that they contradict one another, but both indicate that the dream state may be an important dimension where we experience beings or places that factor into our personal evolution. I asked the same question to Monica's guides and they offered still a different perspective.

JS: Why am I going back there [to that childhood home] so often?

Monica: Because you remember how great your light was at that time, and there's a desire to go back to that time when you may have felt that more. It isn't that your light is any less now; it's like returning to the source. Somehow it represents returning to the source. It was before a time [under her breath] I don't know how to describe this. [Readdressing me.] You became bombarded with other energies, the negativity, and family, and it became more difficult for you to remember your light. And so you go back to that in your sleep to the place where you first felt that light or that peace or whatever aspect of the light where you felt so connected to something.

This description of me returning to the light brings up images of the power station and the line that said, "We provide energy to our extensions and we take information in from the extensions." In other words, our energy goes back and forth between our higher self, the source of our light, and each embodiment of our incarnations. Perhaps I am moving back and forth and connecting to my higher self. In Chapter 8, one of the guides mentioned how we come in with "childlike wonder and innocence," but for most of us, as we are exposed to all aspects of humanity that probably diminishes with time. Perhaps I go there because I desire to experience greater intensity in my light or a stronger connection to Divine light.

The answers to the question about the dreams were varied. Those dreams might provide a portal or a gateway. Perhaps I meet someone there who provides guidance or perhaps it is a way for me to feel and reconnect with my inner light from the power station. Maybe I am not supposed to know the specifics. The most important takeaway was that it appears that our sleep and dream states might be the means by which we can cross dimensions. And, again, I am not implying that this is only something I do. One of the motivations for following up with the dream questions was to obtain more information about how all us may travel or get guidance or reconnect with source energy in the dream state.

As I mentioned earlier, I began this project not really buying into the concept of parallel planes. After being told about a hundred times that I was wrong, with virtually *no* guides offering any sort of support for my misguided view, I had to open myself to alternative possibilities. As I received more information about simultaneous existences, it meant we would have to rethink our conceptual beliefs around how time functions in the Universe.

Apparently, on our planet we have an aquarium in which linear time exists in order for us to learn our lessons. We need to see the consequences of our actions and experience the aging process in order to learn qualities such as empathy and compassion. But linear time is *not* present in many of the other aquariums that contain other dimensions.

Even though it appears that there is a sequence or progression to our lives, the guides—essentially in unanimity—argued that everything is happening in the now. The guidance suggests that moments in our lives that we believe have happened in the past may, in fact, be occurring simultaneously. The same appears to be true with what we call "past lives," which may, in actuality, be concurrent with what we like to think is the present.

Many of the guides said that human minds and human perception may not be able to grasp this alternative construct of time, although several of them tried to come up with some description to help us understand.

Initially, we worked with what I have referred to as an amoebic soul with tentacles that go into lives in simultaneous dimensions. At the end of each tentacle is a "being" having an incarnation. Each of those "beings" is connected to the higher self, and there might be 100 or more of those existences occurring all at the same time.

Then, another more expanded explanation of how time operates in the Universe came forth with the model of the power station. That was the archetype, in which each of our higher selves or soul centers is like a source of energy for our many existences, and it was, for me, the easiest to comprehend and examine.

In that scenario, we send out energy to many different planes of existence, almost like energetic arms where pieces of our soul are undergoing experiential manifestations. At the end of each of those arms, instead of a hand, there is an energetic ball attached, and that energetic ball represents one of our manifestations on that plane. The energy goes back and forth between the power station and the ball of life that is participating in that existence. Those existences may be within this lifetime, within other earthly lifetimes, or within various dimensions, past, present, and future. They are all happening concurrently as there is only now.

We might be able to expand our awareness of these alternative planes through our dream state, through trance states, or through meditation, as it is stillness and the ability to be present that enables us to tap into our higher guidance and experience our connection to Divine energy. Conversely, it is that lack of connection, and lack of being present, as addressed in the next chapter, that makes us feel lost, alone, depressed, and consumed with fear.

One might ask why it is important for us to understand the concept of time. There are a few reasons. First, if we accept the multidimensional nature of the Universe and the idea that we have numerous incarnations, the thought of death becomes far less frightening. If we have hundreds—if not thousands—of other existences, then when we make our transition from this human life, our awareness probably just moves from this life into another incarnation. That incarnation could be an existence back on Earth or on another plane. The guides have likened this process to a natural cycle or rhythm— almost like the rotation of the seasons. As much as some people dread the coming of winter, they always know that spring will come soon thereafter. It is the same thing with death and rebirth into a new consciousness. If we accept that our energy and awareness gently move into another incarnation, it doesn't feel so frightening.

We start anew much like the season of spring returns. But for us to accept this premise, there almost has to be an understanding of time that makes sense to our human minds before we can fully accept that death is not the end and doesn't have to be worrisome or fearful.

When you add to the larger understanding of death the assertion of traveling through incarnations with our soul families, it brings some comfort in that we stay connected to those people we love. We move together through various existences in order to help one another learn and grow.

Perhaps a more important reason for us to understand time and our multidimensional nature is that we might be sharing energy—spirit or higher-self energy—with many other people on this planet. The "flexible arms" coming from that ball of light—our higher-self energy—appear to be everywhere: in many other people, and perhaps even animals, on this planet. There is such interconnectedness that tentacles of our energy may be in lands we never imagined. For example, when you look at a picture of a starving child in a Third World country and it pulls at your heartstrings, that might be because he or she could be sharing energy with you. Or maybe part of your energy is in that child's best friend or mother, and that may be the reason why you felt such empathy when you observed an image of that child.

Conversely, an act of selfishness or terrorism might actually be affecting another spirit part of the person committing that thoughtless deed. What if that terrorist's energy is within one of those people he or she injures in an act of violence? A victim of a bombing might actually contain a connecting soul part that is learning about the consequences of terrorism. That would make sense because nothing happens randomly in the Universe. If the same ball of light is connected to both the terrorist and a victim, it might be the most effective way to convey a lesson and send a forceful message to the higher self.

If we extend this further and include not only our personal numerous incarnations, but also the many simultaneous incarnations of our soul family members, how does that terrorist know that he or she is not blowing up his or her father's spirit or mother's soul part, or perhaps the soul part of a brother, sister, or best friend? The arms of light that run from our higher self to various physical bodies are spread out everywhere and deeply entwined with the arms of light of everyone we know.

The other important implication from this understanding of our interconnected Universe is that absolutely everything we do affects everyone around us. The interconnectedness is far beyond what we ever envisioned. An act of selfishness may hit energetic tentacles we never imagined, just as an act of kindness can affect people in ways we may never know. This model of time illustrates the importance of every action we take. Most of us only think that what we do only affects our immediate world. That is far from the truth.

Chapter 10

# How to Find Love, Connection, and Inner Peace

One of my objectives when I began these *One Voice* dialogues was to gather information that would help people gain a better understanding of the dynamics of the universe. The questions I started out with were designed to elicit answers that would assist the reader in feeling more peaceful about their journey on this planet. In addition to getting general guidance, my hope was that these answers might also benefit those individuals who have felt alone, afraid, sad, angry, or depressed. For example, I asked about what happens when we die because so many individuals are afraid of transition and what will happen when we take our last breath. I asked about the nature of the Divine in order to gather insights for people who were uncertain about spirituality and wanted more information. I asked if our lives were predetermined for those who felt like everything that was happening in their life was out of their control. I asked about soul families so that those individuals who believe they will never see a departed loved one again can feel some comfort in knowing that "loss" isn't forever. I asked what we need to do in order to heal in hopes of helping those who have struggled to manifest good health. And lastly, in the final chapter, I opened up the dialogue so that the guides could share whatever they felt was important in our quest to find inner peace.

We all have moments in which we experience challenges during our journey on this planet, so I wanted to know what might be the best advice for helping us stay on course or, if need be, reconnect with our life purpose. There were eight major recommendations the guides shared that were designed to assist us in releasing our burdens and help us find a true sense of serenity.

The first suggestion came without me broaching any specific topics. In fact, it was something several of the guides brought up on their own volition. The way this came about was that at the end of each session, I would often ask the guides if they had any general advice for people who might be struggling while on their life journey. The most common responses were similar in nature and expressed concern about how we have lost our spiritual connection. Marcus's two spirit guides responded to that question by producing visual images to help illustrate the answer for Marcus.

> JS: Is there anything I didn't ask you that you can offer to help people who feel lost or are struggling that might help them on their journey?
>
> Marcus: I'm just getting a picture that our society as a whole, everybody needs to simplify. Technology is hurting us. As a species, it's hurting our brains. We need to be careful.
>
> JS: How is it hurting our brains?
>
> Marcus: It's fragmenting our brains and keeping them so busy and so fragmented that we can't—it's harder to stay in touch with our spiritual selves. Our spiritual selves are very constant and simple and think clearly and singularly, but

our brains are very fragmented and very scattered because of technology and distractions. With the constant change, people are forgetting about their spirituality.

According to the guides, our brains are being "fragmented" by all of the distractions that come with technology. We have become a society glued to our phones and devices, which makes it impossible for us to be present and in connection with spirit. In some respects, being "connected," as they describe it in the tech world, is actually causing us to disconnect or escape from real life and get lost in an alternate reality. It often prevents us from addressing our issues because it creates a situation in which we can hide from them. It enables us to move through life without paying attention to what we've signed up to do and missing out on the communications we are meant to receive from our guides as they try to direct us on our journeys.

After hearing Marcus's comments, I thought about this new dynamic we've created as a result of our obsession with technology and woke up one morning with the following vision in my head:

*Imagine yourself walking down the bustling streets of a vibrant city on a busy summer afternoon, but your head is consistently looking down at the screen of a mobile device and you're wearing a headset to provide a sound track that keeps you from being present in real time.*

*As you walk down the boulevard, you miss the beautiful music emanating from the open doors of an old stone church. You walk right by the fresh fruit stand where the farmer is selling organic fruit and vegetables and miss out on his feature of the day: fresh, delicious raspberries, rich with flavor. You miss the woman, just down the block, who has a heart attack and the stranger who saves her life with CPR. You don't notice the coffee shop where a voice accompanied by an acoustic guitar sings out about a peaceful revolution. And you never see the radiant being who tries to smile at you even though you are a stranger and the two of you will never cross paths again.*

*And what did you miss? Maybe that stranger with the smile had such radiance and light within her that, for weeks, it would have made you feel happy and alive again. Maybe that music coming from the church was to remind you to start singing again or to meditate or to connect with your guides or to go back to exploring your spiritual path. Maybe sitting at one of those tables in the coffee shop was someone who had the potential to become a lifelong friend. Maybe by witnessing the CPR, it was supposed to be a reminder—a signal from the guides—to go back to the school where you were taking classes in traditional or alternative healing methods. And maybe the fresh raspberries were there to nudge you to start eating healthier or to plant a vegetable garden or to take a day off and go up to the mountains where you could walk along a quiet stream and pick your own wild raspberries.*

*But instead, you walked with your head down and missed it all. The Universe and life was trying to communicate with you, and you weren't present. You missed out on the richness of life so you could watch cat videos or blow up enemy soldiers or check messages or have one of those stimulating "Nothing. What are you doing?" phone conversations.*

There were so many instances in these *One Voice* dialogues in which the guides would say what a privilege it was to be able to have an incarnation on Earth, and yet more and more people have become so fixated on technology that they are missing out on the life experience. It is a choice, and we are not here to tune out the world. That isn't our reason for being on this planet. In fact, it is quite the opposite, and if you are doing that, you are wasting your existence here. Technology is not a substitute for love or connection or real life experience.

I'm not saying we shouldn't use technology, but as with anything else, there must be balance. We are here to be present. If you spend your life engulfed in technology, it is impossible to be present. If we encourage our children to have technology-based lives, they may never learn how to be with real people or how to navigate their own lives. All of this is a choice. Are you choosing to evolve or stay stuck? *Recommendation number one from the guides, when asked about what can help us when we are struggling in life, is to turn off the technology and be present.*

Marcus's guides shared more about the effect technology is having on human beings.

> Marcus: It [technology] is making it so that the brain can't be aware of spirituality anymore. It's harder to reconnect because it keeps everybody's brain in the concrete thoughts rather than being able to feel energy and feeling God as one field. Our brains are so fragmented and thinking of so many things that you can't feel that one feeling anymore.

Our brains are becoming so "fragmented" that we can't feel what we are meant to feel. After hearing these words, it brought to mind an image of being somewhere away from the city lights and looking up at the stars. Many people might stop for a second, gaze up at the sky, and say, "Wow, look at all the stars," but then follow that comment with "I need to get back inside and check my messages," or "Let's go back now and finish that movie we started last night." They don't take the time to stay in the moment, where they sit back and look up at the sky and let their eyes adjust so that the number of stars multiplies by the thousands. They don't take time to find the planets or look for the shapes that make up the constellations. And more importantly, they don't allow themselves to experience and connect with the vast energy that is so present within that moment. That experience of just looking at the stars and the accompanying feeling—perhaps a feeling of peacefulness or stillness—is what we've lost. We don't allow time to simply connect with Divine energy or appreciate how fortunate we are to be experiencing the wonders of this planet. We don't "feel that one feeling anymore."

Marcus's guides weren't the only ones who brought up the impact of technology. In a dialogue with Brooks's angel guide, there was more information about the way technology interferes with our energetic field.

> Brooks: It [technology] is making us less present. We must understand that we are all here to serve in some way. And as we transform through life, and our bodies fall away, then all we have left is the light. The technology is a distraction. It's interfering with our vibrational field, and it's creating anxiety and distraction from our mission, from that which we came to do.

The notion that we are "all here to serve in some way" is about the dharma we build, and that is created through the goodness we bring to the planet and our fellow beings. When "our bodies fall away" and we leave the physical form, "all we have left is the light." In other words, when we make our transition, our guides, angels, soul families, and all of the collective energy that makes up the Divine are not impressed by the video games we played or the number of messages we replied to or, for that matter, even the amount of money we made. None of that is important. Only our light moves to other incarnations and that light becomes more brilliant as a result of the love we share and the kindness we bring to the world. Our existences are about increasing the light within us and the light of the Universe.

The last line from Brooks's angel, "It's interfering with our vibrational field, and it's creating anxiety and distraction from our mission, from that which we came to do," supports the position established in the Chapter 5 about focusing on our lessons. Some individuals jump right in and do their work, but others fail to pay attention, and that avoidance often makes them feel unhappy and unfulfilled. In earlier dialogues, the guides even mentioned how antidepressants can sometimes keep us from addressing what we are here to do. In a sense, those drugs can keep us from dealing with the real world. Technology does the exact same thing. It distracts us from being present with life and provides an escape from facing the issues that we came here to address.

As companies urge us to "stay connected" to the electronic world, it usually comes at the expense of neglecting the spiritual world. In our speeded-up world, we're forgetting the simpler, more natural lifestyle in which we are more present. Mila's angel guide explains:

> Mila: Technology has taken away interconnectedness to the universal energy which is in Earth, which is in living things, animals and people, the processes of the solar system that open us to the processes of the Earth: our seasons, the moon, the tides, water. Technology has just been such a distraction that's created chaos. It's artificial and manufactured chaos. That's what technology is. Because it's simple. It's simple at the end of the day. We eat off the land, we nurture the soil, it feeds us, and that's it. And we live. And that's in the most simplistic terms, but that's not enough. We need to make more meaning. It needs to be more complex, constructed, or chaotic. It's taken away from the very things that brought us here.

There is a stark contrast in that answer between the "chaos" created by our technological world and the "simple" existence and spiritual connectedness we are here to experience. A simple existence is another way of suggesting that we are present and take time to nurture ourselves, whether that is through meditation, preparing and eating healthy meals, or doing things such as taking walks. We are losing our purpose and the more mindful and nurturing aspects of our existence by becoming consumed by a more complex tech world. *Recommendation number two from the guides is to embrace the more mindful and nurturing aspects of our existence.*

Technology adversely affects our energetic vibrations, it keeps us from being present in our lives, and it causes us to neglect both the natural and spiritual world, which is commonly the place we can actually feel at peace. It keeps us from paying attention to our lessons—the very reason we are here on this planet—which commonly leads to anger, depression, and frustration.

We don't need to get rid of technology, but there has to be balance. We aren't supposed to walk down that busy city street and miss everything around us. The Universe is constantly trying to communicate with us, and those individuals with their heads in their devices miss out on everything, including life.

In contrast to our electronic world, when I asked about why we are here, the emphasis was about returning to more uncomplicated lives—focusing on the mindful and nurturing elements—where we are more present. Mila's guide outlines what is necessary for us to have an authentic existence.

JS: Why are we here? What is this journey about for us? What are we learning?

Mila: How to love unconditionally and truthfully. At this point of where we are in humanity, de-evolving, de-evolution. We were evolving so quickly that we thought all the answers were in things, and what we now realize is that we have to take a step back. We have to nurture ourselves. We have to nurture ourselves with little things: cooking for ourselves, taking time to sleep, moving our bodies, getting connected with our soul-source, getting connected with our world and our universe and Earth.

We aren't here to find answers in electronics or material things. Instead, we should be nurturing ourselves with sleep, exercise, mindfulness, and "getting connected with our world and our universe and Earth." This becomes possible by establishing a connection with whatever honors our personal perception of the Divine. It doesn't matter if that connection is with angels, guides, animals, with nature, or in a church, but the remedy and *the third recommen-dation from the guides is to establish a connection with the Divine.*

The guides want to connect with us. They want us to experience their presence and establish a relationship with Divine energy. That doesn't mean we have to go back to formal religion. A spiritual rela-tionship is not about attending church. It is about a personal connec-tion that feels comfortable and natural to your soul. At the end of her session, Shauna, communicating with her spirit guides, gives ad-vice on how to find connection. Once again, this information came after I asked what might help readers of this book.

JS: What have I not asked about that would help people who will read this material?

Shauna: Where to find the teachings. Where do you go?

JS: And what do we tell them for that?

Shauna: You tell them to go into the light. They need to feel the Earth and they need to pray. These places need to be known.

JS: How could a person who is reading this know how to go to the light?

Shauna: You give them direction. You show them the path. It's not always a building that was created. It can be in the forest. It can be in the mountains.

When the guide says "It's not always a building that was created," the implication is that it may or may not be within the walls of a church that was theoretically "created" to provide *direction* to the congregation. Although some individuals might find their spiritual path within a church, some may not. For some, their church may be the forest or the mountains. And for some, it may simply be in a quiet meditation room.

JS: If someone goes to the forest, or imagines in their mind they go to the forest, how do they connect with the light? I'm trying to give the readers a practical way to do this.

Shauna: The light will come to them.

JS: Just ask for the light to come?

Shauna: Yes.

JS: And that light represents?

Shauna: Love, positive energy.

JS: What you're saying is that it may or may not be a church where people find this.

Shauna: No.

JS: Some people may, but some people may not.

Shauna: If you are comfortable in a building, yes.

JS: But for some people...

Shauna [interrupting]: it should be in the open.

JS: For some people, their church might be a waterfall in the forest.

Shauna: Yes.

JS: And that's perfectly fine.

Shauna: Oh, yes.

JS: And they don't need to feel guilty for not following the rules of religion?

Shauna: Right.

In the past, we have been led to believe that if we don't attend church in a formal setting, then we are sinners. The guides want us to know that it is not about the building, the formal setting, the sermons, the dogma, or the sin. The path of spirituality is a very personalized journey and should be comprised of what feels comfortable for each individual. Some will find that path in a church setting, but some won't. Many religions have led us to believe that their way is the only way when, in actuality, the guides keep telling us there are many paths to God.

Establishing a connection is one of the most important tasks on our journey. When we lack a spiritual relationship, we can feel isolated and as if our life lacks direction. I asked Ryan, who was working with Jesus, about ways we can lessen the separation because isolation is one of the most common complaints I hear with clients who feel depressed.

JS: We talked about lessening the separation. What are some ways that people can do that and get back to center, get back to that connectedness?

Ryan: Laughter. Lighten up. Living with joy. Live beyond. Look past simple. Open your eyes to the above. Give all you have to lessening the burdens of others. Enjoy, enjoy, enjoy. We're given everything we can for enjoyment, and you look for the pain and the sorrow and the hurt. Look for the joy, the exuberance, the connection, the love, the distance that is not there, the light that shines always. Don't look at the disaster. Look at the pulling together, the help, the giving, the sharing, the bonding that goes on. Disaster is fleeting. The lesson is beyond that. You focus on the disaster, not the true essence of what's really taking place.

Those words, "Look for the joy, the exuberance, the connection, the love, the distance that is not there, the light that shines always," are a gentle way of suggesting we establish a relationship with the Divine. If you examine the word choices in that passage, many of the words are designed to help us seek out those things that lift up our spirits. We are told to embrace "the joy, the exuberance, the connection, the love." That is an important part of our journey. Conversely, it is the pain, the sorrow, the hurt, and the disasters that take us away from our joy in life. Again, we are being told to be mindful and nurturing. The very things we see on the 5:00 o'clock news and read about online are the things that pull us down energetically and keep us from living with happiness. We can't pretend as if those things don't exist in the world, but as discussed in Chapter 8, we can either give power and energy to the negative aspects of the world, or we can envision and support a world of love, light, and peace.

The last three lines of that passage are especially important. "Disaster is fleeting. The lesson is beyond that. You focus on the disaster, not the true essence of what's really taking place." When we experience a disaster or a crisis in the world, it is easy to focus on the event itself, but if we look closer, at the reaction, that is the "true essence." People rush to the scene to help: some administer first aid, some collect food and donations, some help to rebuild, some come forward to offer counseling and support, some gather together to pray, and so on. This is what Ryan's guide is saying when he says to "Look at the pulling together, the help, the giving, the sharing, the bonding that goes on." As difficult as each disaster may seem, that event creates an opening for a shift in consciousness. Lessons come to us in the form of life challenges, and sometimes those challenges *appear* to be disasters, but our focus should always center on how we can grow and learn from that adversity.

If this sounds like a similar message to the information in Chapter 5 about learning our lessons, it is. On an individual scale, we have challenges and subsequent lessons. On a larger, more global scale, the same dynamic is true for our society, which also goes through difficult times in order for us to grow as a group. There are lessons for each of us on a personal level, and then there are more universal lessons that are designed to help us evolve as a tribe.

When you focus on what can be learned from adversity, you are partnering with the Divine and following the journey you agreed to prior to your incarnation. Each *test* is a part of a plan *you* contracted—either as a sole contractor or as part of a collective— before coming onto this planet. Those who become angry and disconnected from the powers that be, during challenging times, are missing out on the very reason they are here. That disconnect from spirit, which sometimes happens in trying times, can lead to a strong sense of alienation. And that disconnect is often something that has been modeled by the people around us. We've all heard people say things such as: "How could there be a God when all of these bad things keep happening to me?" But because we signed up to experience events that are going to be difficult, we have to decide whether we embrace the lesson or become angry and subsequently isolate ourselves from our spiritual support system. Free will allows us to make that choice.

Our spiritual support system gives us the ability to tap into the oneness, the energy we collectively share. People who feel lonely often lack a genuine connection with spirituality. They might be holding onto some of the pieces of what they had learned in church when they were young, but they don't have that deep bond with the various forms of Divine energy whether that be Source itself or the multitude of guides similar to those represented in this book. Some might ask if there really are guides for all of us. Except for a few resolute individuals who were determined that there would be no guides to work with them in their session, in my experience as a practitioner, guides come forth for most everyone. Even the majority of atheists *are* able to connect with guides in hypnosis. So the ratio of people who are able to work with guides versus those who cannot might be 50 to one. Those who can't are usually those individuals who are unable to fathom the possibility of there being something beyond our physical world. If a person is in a place where they absolutely can't or won't believe something, it is difficult for that to shift. There has to be at least a small degree of open-mindedness or else they will simply generate the outcome they are determined to create. Perhaps a more important question for those individuals is what has made them so resolute in their beliefs and is the position they've taken one that is for their highest good.

Within the context of feeling a lack of connection, the topic of people who experience loneliness came up many times in these dialogues. In the final exchange with Quinn's master guide, I asked for general advice the guide might share with readers, but instead, he wanted to revisit a question I had posed earlier in our discussion about people who feel alone.

JS: Guide, is there anything I didn't ask you feel is important to share that could help people who read this material?

Quinn: Just a little bit about what you just asked me [earlier]. No one is alone. It's a very thin veil between the human experience and the spirit experience, if you will. Very thin veil, and there's always help. And because humans have free will, they do need to ask. It's simple to ask. It doesn't have to be elaborate, just ask.

JS: And how do they do that, in tangible terms?

Quinn: You can say things like, "Show me now what my next step is." You can say, "Please help." It can be real direct and real specific, or it can be general, but you have to engage with us.

JS: And "us" being whom?

Quinn: The guides and spirits and angels, and that energy.

JS: And all of you are dedicated to helping us and guiding us, is that true?

Quinn: Absolutely, and we're never too busy. I think that's the one thing that people think is that they're too busy. We're not too busy.

JS: Do we use that resource enough?

Quinn: No, no.

JS: It sounds like what you're saying is that we're always there, just call on us?

Quinn: Yeah.


Not only is the message that the guides are there for us, but that there is a "very thin veil between the human experience and the spirit experience." Many people feel that the human realm and the spiritual realm are worlds apart. The origin of those beliefs probably goes back to those religions that insisted that God was on one level and humans were on another, far less elevated, level. Contrary to those teachings, the guides talk of our oneness with the Divine to the point where they have told us that we all share energy with one another and with the Divine. They talk of the lack of separation, and their desire to work with us. However, humans "need to ask."

We need to call on them and create a bond with them. That is where free will comes in. We can seek to connect or not connect. That is our option in this lifetime. They can't dictate or will us to work with them. It is our choice.

To make that transition from thinking we are unlovable to knowing we are lovable involves going to the *Source* of unconditional love. *Recommendation number four from the guides is for us to embrace our spiritual nature, which, in turn, opens up the opportunity to feel loved and supported by all manifestations of Divine energy.*

Once we establish a stronger relationship with our guides, we can take advantage of the vast network of encouragement and love from the spiritual realm. I asked Jaden, who was working with a "being of light," about how we can establish a stronger bond to our spiritual nature and, again, the initial response was to see beyond our physical limitations and the constraints of our material world.

JS: For the person who feels lost, how do they get back to this light? What do we do when we are in human form and we want to connect with the spiritual realm?

Jaden: We have to remember we have a spirit. We have to nurture that spirit the way we nurture our bodies. We are so consumed with our bodies. We have to nurture the spirit the way we do the body, and that's how we stay connected to this light. And if we could just be with our spirit, we would tap into this profound energy of the source.

Jaden's guide reminds us that we need to change the focus from our physical bodies and the material world to our spiritual essence. Many of the guides have talked about connecting to the light. The light is the energy of love, but it also represents the oneness or connection we have to all that is in the Universe.

JS: In a practical sense, what are some ways for people here to connect or to get back to that light? You said to nurture; nurture how?

Jaden: Here [referring to our existence on this planet], there are
a thousand ways to distract ourselves from being still with
this light of the spirit within us. And if we can remember to
just be still, then we get in a vibrational alignment with it to
know how to continue to nurture this within us. We move
far faster than this profound light of energy within us. That
[the light] is stillness, quiet, reflection, to just be, and to
really feel this.

When Jaden's guide says "to really feel this," she is referring to the
fact that during her entire session she was experiencing a profound
feeling of light and oneness with the Divine. Her answer, again,
points to the consistencies in these dialogues. First we are reminded
that we are spiritual beings which had been a part of the earlier discussions. Then, once again, we are being told to turn off the distractions. The objective is to be still, quiet, and in reflection: in other
words, be *present*.

JS: So to be in the present, is that what we seem to be losing?

Jaden: Yes. Here [in our physical world] is a place we get so
distracted from this, and that's what we're here to remember;
that we are evolving to a higher level of consciousness to tap
this light of the spirit within us. That's why we're here.

We get distracted or caught up in the day-to-day activities and
forget to be "still" where we can experience "this light of the spirit
within us." Jaden's guide echoes much of what the guides have mentioned earlier about how we can connect with spirit when we are
still or present. When we are focused on things from the past or
what is to come in the future, our energy and attention are consumed by those thoughts and not available to feel the oneness of
the Divine. *Recommendation number five from the guides is to be
present because that is the state in which we are available to share
the feeling of oneness.* The spiritual world is welcoming to all of us,
but the most powerful connections occur when we are fully in the

now, fully aware, and fully tuned-in. It is *not* when we are walking down the city street blindly consumed by what is happening on our devices.

Ben, talking to an archangel, shares the importance of being present with all that is going around us.

> JS: I hear people talk about being in the present, that it is part of a spiritual practice. Why is it important for us to do that?
>
> Ben: The only thing that is current or real is what you have in this very moment that you have your intention or focus on. Everything that you see in the future or past is all in the mind. It is not actually what is so. There's only truth and what is so. There is no truth in the past, and there is no truth in the future because they don't exist.

The last line, "There is no truth in the past, and there is no truth in the future because they don't exist," is interesting. In Chapter 9, time was described as being only "now." Everything is happening in the now. Once again, the difficulty with this concept is that we are undergoing a human experience in which we are subject to the aging process and witness the passage of time. As the guides said in Chapter 9, however, the aging process is only the way it works in "this aquarium." There is the appearance of the passage of time in our world so that we can learn compassion and empathy, but this dynamic does not apply to the greater Universe. In the bigger picture, only the present exists and being in the present opens us up to actively feel and participate in the connection process. When we are consumed by thoughts of the past or the future we become distracted by the material world and are unable to experience the tranquility needed for spiritual expansion.

Another subject that the guides brought up, when asked about what information can help the readers of this book, was their advice on the topic of fear. One of the things that disengages us from being present and existing in a place of connection is our fear and anger. Ben's guide, Archangel Raphael, talks about how this occurs.

JS: What else do people need to know—people who read this book—that would help them raise their vibration?

Ben: There is a very strong addiction in the world as it is today to fear, to the drama that that creates blame, anger. People feel that there is a road somehow if they get mad at the right people, something will alter. It has been said throughout time, in every way, the only way to get to the place of joy is to abandon the addiction to fear and anger. That's where joy lives. Out of joy, your vibration will alter.

The belief that if you get mad or assign blame, then "something will alter" is misguided. The only way to move away from that mindset is to forgive and release what has happened in the past. That enables us to find inner peace again. Archangel Raphael captures that sentiment when he says: "the only way to get to the place of joy is to abandon the addiction to fear and anger."

JS: How has fear and anger gotten so out of control for us?

Ben: It's seductive. It feels powerful. Your societies have created disjointedness where people feel powerless and they clamor for some type of feeling powerful within themselves. It takes telling the truth and being present to see that just like an addict to anything that you have, any of your substances, would tell you, it does seem like that works, but it does not.

Fear and anger might make us feel "powerful" or like we are in control, but that is a delusion. The analogy drawn here is that fear and anger are like an addiction. On some level, we think those qualities put us in control, but they don't. When an individual experiences anger, it is an indication that they have not let go or forgiven the prior damage. It keeps them stuck, makes them fearful that they could attract similar misfortunes in the future, creates a barrier to spiritual connection, and prevents them from making good decisions. How is that being in power? When you look at it logically, it is quite the opposite. Conversely, when that person forgives and releases the past, they take on an aura of love. It is one's loving energy that truly puts an individual in a position of strength. Fear comes from a position of weakness.

I asked Owen's spirit guide about strategies for dealing with fear and this is what his guide had to say.

> JS: What do you say to the person who is in fear? We have a lot of people who are in fear in this world. How do we lessen that fear? What should they do?
>
> Owen: Fear is the absence of love and, if you will, fear is dark, love is light. In subtle ways, doing anything that they love, every day, will help. And I think people have to be willing to share their fear, and talk about their fear, and expose their fear. Once the fear is exposed, it gets completely disengaged. It's in the hiding of the fear, the concealing of the fear, that it gets bigger and bigger and stops people. But voice the fear always, and it completely dissolves.

Owen's guide says "Fear is the absence of love." You can't simultaneously embrace love and fear. Owen's guide also says it is important to talk about fear. Many people believe that getting help or talking to someone is a sign of weakness. On the contrary, addressing our issues is a sign of strength, especially when we are trapped or paralyzed by our negative thoughts. By talking to someone who is neutral to the situation—such as a counselor or therapist—we can process and release the things that make us fearful. *Recommendation number six from the guides is to actively work to release our fears.* It is very likely that addressing fear will be a serious challenge for most individuals, but, again, our challenges are what lead us to uncover our lessons, and focusing on our lessons is why we are here. If fear is presenting itself as an obstacle in one's life, then releasing fear should be the emphasis in order to create positive change.

One of the techniques used for managing fear is to practice being in a place of trust. Trust means that we let go of fear by having confidence that we are safe in the world and anything that happens is always in our highest good. In a sense, we are trusting that our spiritual support system will always be there for us.

> JS: What is the importance of being in a place of trust and how can we use that especially as it relates to fear?

> Ryan: The learning comes from not being separated. Your trust comes from a place of connecting, a place of loving. It comes from being elevated from those who no longer believe. It is the separation that must be overcome. We've answered that the love is all there is. That will overcome separation. Your trust is true because you are not separated. It is the giving of the joy, the laughter, that builds up the others. That can bring them out of the mire, and move up. You, your understanding of your realm, makes you move in the realm you wish.

> JS: So, trust is connection, the opposite of separation?

> Ryan: Correct. Correctly stated. It is the bonding connectedness. It is the absence of singleness that is the trust.

Trust and connection go hand in hand. By trusting, one can "move in the realm you wish," which means that we can exist in a world where we are fully supported by our guides and the Divine. The opposite of trust is control. When we try to control things in life, it is a sign that we are fearful about potential outcomes, and we feel like we must personally take charge. By doing that, we are essentially telling the Divine that we don't trust that energy to support us. We are not trusting the Universe and we are trying to take things in our own hands. As we try to control what happens in our life—a behavior that is predicated by fear—we are alienating ourselves from spirit. We are telling the Universe: I am fearful, I don't trust you, and bad outcomes await me if I don't control everything *and* by being in control I can make sure no challenges—or lessons—come my way. But if lessons help us evolve, trying to constantly be in control can take away the opportunity for a soul to grow.

The most successful course of action is to partner with our Divine guidance instead of sending a message that we don't want their help. Trust is all about embracing the oneness. And though Ryan's reply might sound a bit metaphysical, his guide was Jesus. *Recommendation number seven from the guides is that you can find inner peace and release fear by being in a place of trust.*

Another way to realize inner peace is to practice forgiveness. Without forgiveness, it is nearly impossible to be present and connected because non-forgiveness means we are holding onto our old issues. Audrey, working with a spirit guide, explains:

JS: How important is forgiveness as a way to elevate our consciousness?

Audrey: Forgiveness is the ultimate act of love of self. God is always love and forgiveness. God always forgives. It is humans that don't understand that. If we can apply forgiveness, self-forgiveness, forgiveness of others, it's the ultimate application of love to the self.

JS: And that elevates our consciousness and we become closer to that Divine energy?

Audrey: Yes, it's like you let love in. More love, less fear, higher consciousness.

One of the common misconceptions about forgiveness is that it benefits those responsible for the negative actions. It is actually the exact opposite. It aids the individual doing the forgiveness. When we forgive, it is the "ultimate application of love to the self." By forgiving, we release the emotional charge we are holding. That charge might be fear, anger, hurt, shame, embarrassment, or any of a number of issues or emotions. Through forgiveness, we are releasing ourselves from the people and events that might otherwise keep us living in the past and, in turn, that action enables us to spiritually evolve to a state of "higher consciousness" and inner peace.

Forgiveness is also important because it is an acknowledgment that we are all here to learn. In order to learn, we all are going to make mistakes and make bad choices. That is an essential part of the life journey. None of us are perfect, and many of the "bad things" that happen *to us* are actually events we *chose* to experience—and were meant to occur—because that is part of our learning process. Melinda's angel explains:

JS: How important is forgiveness?

Melinda: It is the key to everything. Forgiveness is the only way. It is the only way that you have full growth. It is the only way that you have full freedom. Forgiveness of yourself, forgiveness to yourself, and forgiveness to others. The point of life isn't to be perfect. The point of life is not to never make a mistake. The point of life isn't: I followed all the rules perfectly and now I'm being rewarded. The purpose of life is to learn, and as you learn, you realize there is absolutely no point in carrying over resentment or anger because everybody's learning. If somebody makes a mistake or expresses something that is negative to you, for you to hold onto that and to blame them for that is perpetuating. It's perpetuating. They're learning as well. It doesn't mean you have to make it okay, but to forgive them is to free yourself. And to forgive yourself is where true freedom and true peace are.

To forgive is "to free yourself." Holding on with non-forgiveness is "perpetuating," which means that it can continue to indefinitely block you from freedom, from inner peace, and from growth. The person withholding absolution remains stuck, unable to fully experience their spiritual potential. Because of the lessons we have here in Earth's classroom, we may have agreed to participate in negative experiences, and it is through those events that we learn. If we choose *not* to process or forgive those experiences that make up our lessons, then we are interfering with our opportunity to learn.

In the larger picture, forgiveness is a major part of our spiritual journey. Melinda's angel went on to share how important forgiveness is on a more Universal scale.

Melinda: If you feel your sins will never be forgiven or that you carry an original sin by virtue of being you, it is okay to release those beliefs. Naturally, this isn't a free pass where you can commit whatever sins you choose without a conscience: individuals who do that are harming their spiritual essence and moving away from that blissful connection of pure love and light. But for those who carry the burden of a long ago discretion and are convinced, even after years of remorse, that they can never be set free, the guides want you to understand that Divine energy can and will forgive you. If that is impossible to obtain with your church, then you might have to explore new paths of spirituality.

The first part of this message tells us that if we have done something wrong in life or believe that we "carry an original sin," it is okay to forgive yourself. The old conviction that a sin is a black mark that remains forever on your soul is one of those beliefs tied into faiths that reside in a dynamic of punishment and non-forgiveness. The guides are saying that it is acceptable for you to let go of or "release those beliefs." Remember: the essence of the Universe is, and has always been, love and forgiveness.

The other part of this message makes it clear that there are no free passes when sins are committed without a conscience. We already know from earlier dialogues that the Universe is not set up so that people who do bad things receive some form of horrific karmic retribution. Instead, Melinda's angel tells us that those who do unconscionable acts are "harming their spiritual essence and moving away from that blissful connection of pure love and light." That may not sound serious, but it is. If one intentionally hurts others, they are effectively harming the fate of their own spirit. Never being able to feel "love and light" could potentially mean moving through eternity stuck in a dark, negative existence. *Recommendation number eight from the guides is that forgiveness brings us more in line with our higher spiritual essence.*

One of the main objectives of the guides during these dialogues was to help us establish a more powerful spiritual connection. In order to do that, we have to release many of our human foibles. In other words, we have to let go of our humanness and embrace the fact that we are, first and foremost, spiritual beings. The more we resonate with our spiritual essence, the more our existence becomes filled with love, joy, happiness, and peace. The guides had eight areas where they advised us on how to facilitate our spiritual growth. If we look at the recommendations from the guides, they break down like this:

- Turn off the technology and be present.
- Practice the more mindful and nurturing aspects of our existence.
- Establish a connection with the Divine.
- Embrace our spiritual nature and open up to the love and support offered by all manifestations of Divine energy.
- Be present because that is the state in which we are available to share the feeling of oneness.
- Actively work to release our fears.
- Approach life from a place of trust.
- Practice forgiveness as it allows us to embrace our spiritual essence.

Sometimes it is difficult to make changes like this, but as we do our work, there are no deadlines and there is no failure. The guides are *always* there to support you. It is not about perfection, only intent. Whenever we try to move in a positive direction, we are evolving. Most of us won't "fix" everything in this lifetime, and that is perfectly fine. We do what we can, and it is important to remember that the guides love us no matter what.

As the goal of this chapter was about establishing spiritual connection, I wanted to end with a client trying her best to describe what that connection felt like to her. I suspect that what we feel in our human bodies might pale in comparison to what true spiritual essence is really like. Still, it is exhilarating, and at the end of each *One Voice* session, I tried to give each client the opportunity to *feel* Divine energy. Bree, working with her angel guide, described what the experience was like for her. Most clients had difficulty finding the right words to express the sensation, but Bree did her best to help the readers appreciate the intensity of the vibration of Spirit.

JS: As you feel the energy of or vibration of these beings of light, what is it like?

Bree: I feel nothing. I have no thoughts. Everything is pure. Everything is clean and pure. There is no anything. It is open.

JS: How does it feel for you?

Bree: Free, and simple, and light.

JS: Why is this important for you to feel this?

Bree: This is my truth. This is my truth and my path to understand the Divine, and understand God's role in my life. All the questions I've asked and all the seeking is to get to this point. There's no roller coaster anymore. It is fluid. It is so trusting. It is not artificial. It's an essence that is just truth. There's no other way to explain it. There's no way to manufacture it or artificially create it. It's just being. It is truth, it is hope, it is love, it is joy, and it is peace, actually a lot of peace.

JS: Is this experience what it means to be present? Is that what this is?

Bree: Because there is no before, there is no after, there is no thought. It is hard for me to articulate it because you're in it. There isn't any description. It is now. It is the moment. It is this.

JS: So it's [is it similar to] being in the moment and being in trust?

Bree: It's higher. It's the higher source. It's completely trusting in the higher source, and knowing, and not telling yourself you know, that knowing with every ounce of your being that everything's fine. Everything's exactly the way it should be. Nothing is out of place. Nothing is missing. You're not looking for anything. You're not trying to discover anything.

JS: How does that feel in your mind and body and spirit?

Bree: Connected. Connected and free in peace.

JS: Is this a good place for you to go?

Bree: It is a place of awesome.

In contrast to all of this discussion about disconnection, it is interesting to hear what it feels like to be fully present and be fully connected. We can talk about it conceptually, but it helps to have it expressed by someone undergoing the connection experience. Many clients who tried to describe what they felt reflected similar sentiments, but most found it difficult to explain the sensations because of the limitations we have with the English language. The important takeaway from this account is that this spiritual support system is available to each and every one of us. In fact, all of this amazing information—the wisdom of the guides—is, I believe, their way of trying to reach out to us as we attempt to navigate our way through life on this planet.

# Conclusion

When I began this project, I didn't set out to try to convert readers to a specific belief system or convince them that my opinions on spirituality were the ones that they should embrace. In fact, it was quite the opposite. To use the old cliché: I didn't have a horse in the race. I wasn't motivated by an overt—or covert—intention of convincing readers that they needed to follow my beliefs. In fact, on many of these topics, instead of having preconceived ideas I wanted to promote, I truly didn't know what to expect. I didn't know what the guides were going to say. I have described the process as a journey of discovery because it was a progression of unearthing new information, much like an archeological dig in which I was piecing together artifacts in order to understand concepts or, in this case, a paradigm that I never fully understood.

As I learned new things, I was excited about sharing that information. I tried to process or decipher the material and in some cases relate it to my life experiences because that made it more relevant for me and, hopefully, more accessible for the reader.

There were several occasions in which I was surprised along the way. For example, when I started out, I didn't support the notion of parallel dimensions and certainly had no conceptual blueprint of how that could be possible. I wanted to believe that karma would rain down on bad people and they would be held responsible for their deeds. I really wasn't sure if there was such a thing as evil, so that became a topic I put on the table in hopes of gaining insight. Each new topic became a new learning experience.

Along the way, I was amazed by the incredible cohesion within the answers. There was a flow to the communication: one answer supported the next. For example, the conceptual model of time fittingly came right after the discussions about multiple and simultaneous existences, and it effectively tied all of that material together. Instead of having the guidance feel like it was coming from dozens and dozens of random sources—and from a diverse group of people who didn't know one another—it was as if all of the information perfectly fit together and was all coming from a single source, from *one voice*.

What do we do with this new information? There might be some things we want to approach differently, but not everything has to change. Some readers, for instance, might be wondering if the new information we learned in these dialogues means that they need to rethink their spiritual beliefs. For example, someone who feels a strong connection with Jesus might be asking themselves if it is possible to maintain that relationship in light of new information about multiple incarnations or soul families. Someone else might wonder if they can continue to pray to God or Allah or Buddha when the guides have told us the Divine is actually energy.

For those who feel perfectly aligned with their spirituality, those comfortable beliefs don't have to change. There are many paths that connect with the Divine, and in no way did the guides ever say to abandon what is important to you. True spirituality is very personal and is predicated much more on how you live your life than what house of worship you attend. If you approach everything in your life from a place of love and light, then it makes no difference if that inspiration comes from Jesus, Mary, Allah, Buddha, or from Earth energy. All of those are sources of love and light, and the guides *never* tried to tell anyone which one they should choose.

So, if you feel an incredible love and connection with Jesus, please don't let any of the wisdom here take that away. If you feel a connection to the Earth and the animals and the Great Spirit, please add this new knowledge and guidance to that journey, but don't feel that your way isn't correct. If you are Muslim and pray to Allah every day and that allows you to feel joy and gives you the guidance you need to bring love and light to the world, then please keep up the good work. If you have a minister or rabbi or priest that you enjoy, then absolutely continue to attend that service. If you belong to a church where you feel a sense of connection and the congregants there have become like family, then that is the perfect place for you. The purpose of this book is not to take away genuine spiritual connections; it is to build on them and to help you navigate this earthly experience in a way where you leave this planet with an essence of love and kindness.

The key to spirituality is following what feels true to your heart. The approach of the guides was supportive and gentle. They didn't tell us to what to do, just as other humans shouldn't *tell* us what to do. The guides simply questioned any dogma and doctrines that might not be serving us. We no longer need to accept the beliefs that others might have imposed in the past. Spirituality is a very personal path and what works for one may not be right for others. We have reached a point in our evolution where it is perfectly appropriate to let go of beliefs that others have thrust upon us, especially when that is done through guilt, fear, or some form of coercion. If you are being pressured by your church, don't feel you belong, don't agree with their teachings, or feel you've become an outcast because of their rules, then it is okay to explore other approaches that might be more in line with what feels right to you.

What should change based on what the guides have told us in these conversations? It isn't so much about making drastic changes as perhaps assimilating new information into our consciousness.

The guides want us to know that there is no judgment or hierarchy when it comes to who is most deserving of Divine love and acceptance. We are all loved to a degree that is unfathomable to the human mind. There are no exceptions or exclusions to this. The nature of the Universe and Divine energy *is* loving and forgiving. There is incredible spiritual support from guides, angels, spirit animals, light workers, healers, religious figures such as Jesus and Buddha, and many other forms of Divine energy. They want you to connect with them. They want to help you and guide you. Whether you use prayer, meditation, self-hypnosis, or just quiet time, they want to establish a relationship in which they can give you love and support.

We are here to learn lessons. That is part of our journey. Some of those lessons are tough. If you ignore them, they will keep presenting themselves until you pay attention. Denial and prescription drugs are not methods to deal with your lessons. It is quite the opposite. That is a way of ignoring your lessons, and the guides say that people who do this often fall into unpleasant emotional states and may manifest physical disharmonies connected to lesson avoidance.

The "bad things" that happen in our lives are incidents we agreed to before we incarnated in order to learn those lessons. Those "bad things" are never done to punish, only educate, and there is never a time—under any circumstances—when anything is done to us because we are unloved or rejected.

There is no hell and no devil. If you feel overwhelmed or afraid because of the concept of hell, then it is okay to walk away from those beliefs that don't serve you. Our purpose on this planet is to work through our fears, not to live in a perpetual state of fear.

The guides want you to know that you don't have to be afraid of dying. Your soul is immortal. You *never* die, only the physical body wears out and fades away. We have so many existences that the guides have said it is incomprehensible to the human mind. If you have thousands of lives, perhaps hundreds happening simultaneously to the one you are having now, losing one isn't something to be in fear about.

Those people who are close to us are our soul family members. You will be with them in many, many existences. When one of them transitions from this earthly plane, they are still with you and will probably be with you for a long, long time. They—the guides and the person who made their transition—don't want you to stop living your life or go into a long period of depression or fear. They want you to live and learn and experience joy.

Turn off the technology. Turn off the phones, the tablets, the computers, the televisions, and let yourself be. Find a place of balance in our modern world through moderation, not overindulgence. Every single action around you is there for you to learn something new, so pay attention. Technology is distracting us from our spiritual journey.

We are on this planet to thrive and learn. As you experience the Creator, creating through you, make this journey one of light and love. Let it be a journey where you create beauty and spread joy. Leave only footprints: make the Earth and the people on the planet a better place because of your presence.

Emanate a consciousness of unconditional love and forgiveness. If every day, every being on the planet projected love, light, and forgiveness to every soul on the planet, we have the potential to change the collective consciousness.

Finally, as I bring this venture to a close, I wanted to include an excerpt from a dialogue with group of guides who changed the commonly practiced pattern I'd used during these interviews: in this instance, they had a message they wanted to share directly with me. The question that prompted this communication was when I asked those guides what other information they could share during the interview that might help people on their path. Their response turned the focus back to the purpose of this book.

JS: What have I not asked that could be important to share with people who read this book? What else do people know that could be beneficial?

Elise: How do you want them to feel when they read your book?

JS: Like there's hope, like they have some direction.

Elise: Direction, hope, guidance, then as you write, you infuse your book with those qualities and as you think about the human beings that are going to pick your book above all others from the bookshelf or from the online shopping, then you think about them and you envision them holding it with hope and holding it with the wisdom of guidance and allowing your words to convey that.

So, I finish this journey of discovery with my intention for all of you and for all of humanity. My hope is that the wisdom from the guides may bring comfort and peace and inspiration to those who are seeking answers. My hope is for those who feel lost to know that they are loved and there is an incredible network of spiritual support for every single person on this planet. My hope is for every soul to embrace its inner radiance. And more than anything, my hope for the Earth, and all of the beings who walk this Earth, is that we join together to create a world of love and light.

# Afterword

One of the questions that arose during the course of writing this book was whether or not this process was completely unique to my practice or if it could be duplicated by another hypnotherapist. We have started to discover that when an individual conducts an experiment, their very presence and energy field can often influence the results of that experiment. Was that the case with these clients who were able to communicate with their guides?

That was an important issue, so I contacted a colleague who is very skilled in the art of hypnosis to see if the guides were willing to share in a context where another individual was acting as the administrator. I gave her a series of questions similar to some of those I had used in the research for this book:

&#8269; Is there such a thing as God or Divine or Universe or whatever description you want to use, and if so, what is the essence or nature of the Divine?

&#8269; What happens when we die?

&#8269; Do we stay connected to those people who we are close to in this lifetime?

&#8269; Why are we here on this planet?

&#8269; Is there just one time on this planet or do we have other existences?

We brought in a new set of clients and had them work with my colleague and found that, indeed, we were able to create the same dynamic and get the same type of responses that occurred within the *One Voice* dialogues.

The only caution I would pass on to the reader is that working within other realms, visiting other dimensions, and exploring past and present lives should only be done with a hypnotist who is certified, experienced, and trained in this type of work. This should *not* be attempted by those who dabble or experiment with hypnosis, nor should it be administered by those who are not deftly experienced in guiding clients through other realms and handling situations that can sometimes trigger very emotional reactions. I also caution readers *not* to agree to be hypnotized by someone who does not have the appropriate credentials and proper training.

In the future, I hope to train other hypnotists in these methods, and once that is in place, you can consult my Website at the Rocky Mountain Hypnotherapy Center (*www.rmhypnotherapy.com*) to find a hypnotist in your area who I recommend for this work.

This form of alchemical hypnotherapy is extremely exciting. The process can be life-changing and has the potential to raise the collective consciousness of the entire planet. I am eternally grateful for the participants in these dialogues as well as the guides who graciously shared such amazing information. Each of you contributed to the healing of humankind as well as the healing of our planet. Many blessings to each and every one of you.

# Index

# About the Author

James Schwartz, BCH, is a Board Certified Hypnotherapist and an NLP practitioner. He is certified by the National Guild of Hypnotists and is a member of the Colorado Association of Psychotherapists. James is the founder and director of the Rocky Mountain Hypnotherapy Center in Lakewood, Colorado, and is certified in Complementary Medical Hypnosis, NeuroLinguistic Programming, and HypnoBirthing. He is a graduate of California State University, Dominguez Hills and San Diego State University. James is a former teacher of English and has taught a vast array of subjects including courses on Writing for Multimedia, ESL, Meditation, and Hypnosis to Promote Fertility.

Through his extensive work with infertility clients, James created and developed the Hypnosis to Promote Fertility program, which focuses on healing the mental and emotional barriers that can often prevent conception. This work led to his book, *The Mind-Body Fertility Connection*, which was endorsed by leaders in the fields of acupuncture, psychotherapy, hypnotherapy, and Maya massage.

*One Voice, Sacred Wisdom* is a groundbreaking exploration into the communications we are receiving from other realms. Through the use of alchemical hypnosis, James was able to receive information about life, death, the afterlife, karma, parallel planes, healing, and why we exist on this planet from clients who were communicating directly with their guides.

You can contact the author through the website for The Rocky Mountain Hypnotherapy Center, LLC, at *www.rmhypnotherapy.com* or by going to the website for the book, which you can find at *www.onevoicesacredwisdom.com/.*

## Other Books by James Schwartz

*The Mind-Body Fertility Connection*